HANDEL

Samson

An oratorio for soprano, alto, tenor & bass soli,
SATB & orchestra

The piano accompaniment revised from that of the German Handel Society

Order No: NOV 070144

NOVELLO PUBLISHING LIMITED
8/9 Frith Street, London W1V 5TZ

PREFACE.

It nas often been felt as an inconvenience that while none of Handel's oratorios (with the exception of "Israel in Egypt") are ever performed in their entirety, all editions of the scores give the complete works, rendering it at times difficult for hearers to follow the music, in consequence of the frequent omissions of numbers, either in whole or in part.

The present edition of "Samson," prepared in the first instance for the Leeds Musical Festival of 1880, contains only those portions of the music which were given on that occasion. With the exception of two numbers (No. 38 and No. 78), the selection is the same as that used by the Sacred Harmonic Society, and at most provincial performances. The curtailments in the recitatives were in many cases made by Handel himself in performance (see Preface to the German Handel Society's edition of "Samson"), while in others they are sanctioned by long custom. In one recitative, "Brethren, and men of Dan" (No. 17), it has been necessary to transpose the music a tone lower, in order to form a suitable connection with the following number.

SAMSON.

PERSONS REPRESENTED.

SAMSON.
MICAH, *his friend.*
MANOAH, *his father.*
DALILA, *his wife.*
HARAPHA, *a Giant of Gath.*
ISRAELITISH MESSENGER.
ISRAELITISH WOMAN.
PRIESTS OF DAGON.
VIRGINS, *attendant upon Dalila.*
ISRAELITES, *friends of Samson.*
ISRAELITISH VIRGINS.
PHILISTINES.

ARGUMENT.

PART I.—Samson, blind and captive to the Philistines, being relieved from his toil by a Festival in honour of Dagon their god, comes forth into the open air.—The Priests of Dagon sing in praise of their idol.—Samson, bemoaning his condition, is visited by his friends and his father Manoah, who join in bewailing his degradation.—Samson, acknowledging the justice of his punishment, predicts that Dagon will not be allowed to triumph over the God of Israel.—Samson, however, declares his hopes to be gone, his nature declining, and his life drawing to a close.—Upon which his friends recount to him the joy and peace that his spirit will realise in the eternal world.

PART II.—Micah and the Israelites call upon God to have pity on Samson.—Dalila, his wife, then appears, and pretending penitence and submission, entreats him to go home with her. He refuses to listen to her entreaties; a scene of mutual recrimination ensues, and they separate. His friends assert the ordained subjection of the wife to the husband.—Harapha, a giant of Gath, then approaches, attracted by the fame of Samson's prodigious might, and boasts how he would have overcome him had he encountered him before his captivity.—Samson dares him to a trial now, which he refuses, and is taunted by Samson with cowardice.—Micah proposes, as a test of who is the supreme God, that Harapha should call upon Dagon to try his power over Samson.—The Israelites prostrate themselves before Jehovah, and supplicate His delivering aid.—Harapha calls upon Dagon, and the worshippers of that idol appeal to him for protection and succour; after which, the Israelites and Philistines jointly, but in opposition to each other, celebrate the majesty, power, and supremacy of their respective deities.

PART III.—Harapha is sent by the Philistine lords to bid Samson attend their festival, to exhibit his strength before them, which at first he refuses to do. His friends, perplexed for his safety, call upon God for help.—Samson, persuaded inwardly that this was from God, yields to go along with Harapha, who comes again with great threatenings to fetch him.—Samson departs, invoking the aid of that Spirit with which he had formerly been inspired.—His friends cheer him on, and declare him to be fulfilling the call, and under the guidance of Heaven. Manoah returns to tell his friends his hopes of obtaining Samson's release. The Priests of Dagon are heard to celebrate the praises of their idol for subduing their foe.—Micah and Manoah hear the shouts of joy, and the latter again manifests his paternal solicitude for Samson. An appalling, loud, and confused noise is heard, succeeded by wailings and cries for help.—An Israelitish messenger arrives in breathless haste, and relates to the relations and friends of Samson the fearful news of his having pulled down the Philistine temple, and buried his enemies and himself in its ruins.—Micah and the Israelites lament his fall.—A Dead March is heard, and his body approaches on its way to the tomb; and Manoah and Micah and the Israelites perform the funeral rites.

PART THE FIRST.

OVERTURE.

SCENE.—*Before the Prison in Gaza.*

SAMSON, *blind and in chains. Attendant leading him.*

RECITATIVE.

Samson.

This day, a solemn feast to Dagon held
Relieves me from my task of servile toil;
Unwillingly their superstition yields
This rest, to breathe heav'n's air, fresh blowing, pure, and sweet.

Enter a troop of the PRIESTS *and* WORSHIPPERS *of* DAGON, *celebrating his festival.*

CHORUS.

Priests, &c.

Awake the trumpet's lofty sound;
The joyful sacred festival comes round,
When Dagon king of all the earth is crown'd.

AIR.

Philistine Woman.

Ye men of Gaza, hither bring
The merry pipe and pleasing string,
The solemn hymn, and cheerful song;
Be Dagon prais'd by every tongue.

CHORUS.

Awake the trumpet's lofty sound;
The joyful sacred festival comes round,
When Dagon king of all the earth is crown'd.

RECITATIVE.

Samson.

Why by an Angel was my birth foretold,
If I must die betray'd, and captiv'd thus,
The scorn and gaze of foes? O cruel thought,
My griefs find no redress; they inward prey,
Like gangren'd wounds, immedicable grown.

Micah.

Matchless in might! once Israel's glory, now her grief!
We come (thy friends well known) to visit thee.

Samson.

Welcome, my friends!

Micah.

Which shall we first bewail, thy bondage or lost sight?

Samson.

Oh, loss of sight! of thee I most complain.
Oh, worse than beggary, old age, or chains!
My very soul in real darkness dwells!

AIR.

Total eclipse! no sun, no moon,
All dark amidst the blaze of noon!
O glorious light! no cheering ray
To glad my eyes with welcome day!
Why thus depriv'd thy prime decree?
Sun, moon, and stars are dark to me.

CHORUS.

Israelites.

O first-created beam, and Thou, great Word,
Let there be light! and light was over all;
One heav'nly blaze shone round this earthly ball,
To Thy dark servant life by light afford.

Manoah.

Brethren and men of Dan, say where 's my son
Samson, fond Israel's boast? Inform my age.

Micah.

As signal now in low dejected state,
As in the height of pow'r: see where he lies;

RECITATIVE (accompanied).

Manoah.

The good we wish for often proves our bane;
I pray'd for children, and I gained a son,
And such a son, as all men hail'd me happy;
But who'd be now a father in my stead?
The blessing drew a scorpion's tail behind:
This plant, select and sacred, for awhile
The miracle of men, was in an hour
Ensnar'd, assaulted, overcome, led bound,
His foes' derision, captive, poor and blind.

AIR.

Thy glorious deeds inspir'd my tongue,
Whilst airs of joy from thence did flow;
To sorrows now I tune my song,
And set my harp to notes of woe.

RECITATIVE (accompanied).

Samson.

Justly these evils have befall'n thy son.
Sole author I, sole cause.
My grief for this forbid mine eyes to close, or thoughts to rest:
But now the strife shall end; me overthrown,
Dagon presumes to enter lists with God;
Who thus provok'd will not connive, but rouse
His fury soon, and His great Name assert.
Dagon shall stoop, ere long be quite despoil'd
Of all those boasted trophies won on me.

AIR.

Why does the God of Israel sleep?
Arise with dreadful sound,
With clouds encompass'd round,
Then shall the heathen hear Thy thunder deep.

The tempest of Thy wrath now raise,
In whirlwinds them pursue.
Full fraught with vengeance due,
Till shame and trouble all Thy foes shall seize.

CHORUS.

Israelites.

Then shall they know that He, whose Name
Jehovah, is alone
O'er all the earth, but One,
Was ever the Most High, and still the same

RECITATIVE.

Manoah.

For thee, my dearest son—must thou meanwhile
Lie, thus neglected, in this loathsome plight.

Samson.

It should be so. Why should I live?
Soon shall these orbs to double darkness yield.
My genial spirits droop, my hopes are fled;
Nature in me seems weary of herself;
My race of glory run, and race of shame,
Death, invocated oft, shall end my pains,
And lay me gently down with them that rest.

CHORUS.

Israelites.

Then round about the starry throne
Of Him who ever rules alone,
Your heavenly guided soul shall climb;
Of all this earthly grossness quit,
With glory crown'd for ever sit,
And triumph over Death, and thee, O time!

PART THE SECOND.

SCENE.—*The same.*

SAMSON, MICAH, *and* ISRAELITES.

RECITATIVE.

Samson.

My evils hopeless are, one pray'r remains,
A speedy death to close my miseries.

Micah.

Relieve Thy champion, image of Thy strength,
And turn his labours to a peaceful end.

AIR.

Return, O God of Hosts! behold
Thy servant in distress,
His mighty griefs redress,
Nor by the heathen be they told.

CHORUS.

Israelites.

To dust his glory they would tread,
And number him amongst the dead.

RECITATIVE.

Micah.

But who is this, that so bedeck'd and gay,
Comes this way sailing like a stately ship?
'Tis Dalila, thy wife.

Samson.

My wife? my traitress! let her not come near me.

Dalila.

With doubtful feet, and wav'ring resolution,
I come, O Samson, dreading thy displeasure;
But conjugal affection led me on,
Prevailing over fear and timorous doubt.
Glad if in aught my help or love could serve to expiate my rash, unthought misdeed.

AIR.*

Dalila.

With plaintive notes and am'rous moan,
Thus coos the turtle left alone.

AIR.

My faith and truth, O Samson, prove;
But hear me, hear the voice of love;
With love no mortal can be cloyed,
All happiness is love enjoyed.

CHORUS.

Virgins.

Her faith and truth, O Samson, prove,
But hear her, hear the voice of love.

RECITATIVE.

Samson.

Ne'er think of that, I know thy warbling charms,
Thy trains, thy wiles, and fair enchanted cup.
Their force is null'd. Where once I have been caught,
I shun the snare. These chains, this prison-house,
I count the house of liberty to thine.

* This is omitted.

DUET.

Dalila.

Traitor to love, I'll sue no more
For pardon scorned, your threats give o'er.

Samson.

Traitress to love, I'll hear no more
The charmer's voice, your arts give o'er.

[*Exeunt* DALILA *and* VIRGINS.

RECITATIVE.

Samson.

Favour'd of heaven is he who finds one true;
How rarely found!—his way to peace is smooth.

CHORUS.

Israelites.

To man God's universal law
Gave pow'r to keep his wife in awe;
Thus shall his life be ne'er dismay'd,
By female usurpation sway'd.

RECITATIVE.

Micah.

No words of peace, no voice enchanting fear,
A rougher tongue expect,—here 's Harapha,
I know him by his stride and haughty look.

Enter HARAPHA *and* PHILISTINES.

Harapha.

I come not, Samson, to condole thy chance;
I am of Gath, men call me Harapha:
Thou know'st me now; of thy prodigious might
Much have I heard, incredible to me!
In this displeas'd, that never in the field
We met, to try each other's deeds of strength:
I'd see if thy appearance answers loud report.

Samson.

The way to know, were not to see, but taste.

Harapha.

Ha! dost thou then already single me?
I thought that labour and thy chains had tamed thee.
Had fortune brought me to that field of death,
Where thou wrought'st wonders with an ass's jaw,
I 'd left thy carcase where the ass lay dead.

Samson.

Boast not of what thou would'st have done, but do.

Harapha.

The honour certain to have won from thee
I lose, prevented by thy eyes put out;
To combat with a blind man I disdain.

AIR.

Honour and arms scorn such a foe,
Tho' I could end thee at a blow,
Poor victory, to conquer thee,
Or glory in thy overthrow:
Vanquish a slave that is half slain!
So mean a triumph I disdain

Samson.

Cam'st thou for this, vain boaster? yet take heed;
My heels are fettered, but my hands are free.
Thou bulk of spirit void, I once again,
Blind, and in chains, provoke thee to the fight.

Harapha.

O Dagon! can I hear this insolence,
To me unused, not rendering instant death!

DUET.

Samson.

Go, baffled coward, go,
Lest vengeance lay thee low;
In safety fly my wrath with speed.

Harapha.

Presume not on thy God,
Who under foot has trod
Thy strength and thee, at greatest need.

RECITATIVE.

Micah.

Here lies the proof;—if Dagon be thy god,
With high devotion invocate his aid.
His glory is concerned; let him dissolve
Those magic spells that gave our hero strength:
Then know whose god is God; Dagon of mortal make,
Or that Great One whom Abram's sons adore.

CHORUS.

Israelites.

Hear, Jacob's God, Jehovah, hear!
O save us, prostrate at Thy throne!
Israel depends on Thee alone;
Save us, and show that Thou art near.

RECITATIVE.

Harapha.

Dagon, arise, attend thy sacred feast;
Thy honour calls, this day admits no rest.

CHORUS.

Philistines.

To song and dance we give the day,
Which shows thy universal sway.
Protect us by thy mighty hand,
And sweep this race from out the land.

CHORUS.

Israelites and Philistines.

Fixed in His everlasting seat,
Jehovah / Great Dagon } rules the world in state.
His thunder roars, heaven shakes, and earth 's aghast.
The stars, with deep amaze,
Remain in stedfast gaze;
Jehovah / Great Dagon } is of Gods the first and last.

PART THE THIRD.

SCENE.—*The same.*

SAMSON, MICAH, *and* ISRAELITES.

RECITATIVE.

Micah.

More trouble is behind; for Harapha
Comes on amain, speed in his steps and look.

Samson.

I fear him not, nor all his giant brood.

Enter HARAPHA.

Harapha.

Samson, to thee our lords thus bid me say:
"This day to Dagon we do sacrifice
With triumph, pomp, and games; we know thy strength
Surpasses human rate; come, then, and show
Some public proof, to grace this solemn feast."

Samson.

I am an Hebrew, and our law forbids
My presence at their vain religious rites.

Harapha.

This answer will offend; regard thyself.

Samson.

Myself! my conscience and internal peace!
Am I so broke with servitude, to yield
To such absurd commands? to be their fool,
And play before their god? I will not come.

Harapha.

My message, given with speed, brooks no delay.

AIR.

Presuming slave! to move their wrath;
For mercy sue,
Or vengeance due
Dooms in one fatal word thy death:
Consider, ere it be too late
To ward th' unerring shaft of fate.

[*Exit.*

RECITATIVE.

Micah.

Consider, Samson, matters now are strain'd
Up to the height, whether to hold or break.
He 's gone, whose malice may inflame the lords.

Samson.

Shall I abuse this consecrated gift
Of strength, again returning with my hair,
By vaunting it in honour to their god,
And prostituting holy things to idols?

Micah.

How thou wilt here come off surmounts my reach;
'Tis heaven alone can save both us and thee.

CHORUS.

Israelites.

With thunder armed, great God, arise;
Help, Lord, or Israel's champion dies;
To Thy protection this Thy servant take,
And save, O save us, for Thy servant's sake.

RECITATIVE.

Samson.

Be of good courage; I begin to feel
Some secret impulse, which doth bid me go.

Micah.

In time thou hast resolved, again he comes.

Enter HARAPHA.

Harabha.

Samson, this second message send our lords;
"Haste thee at once, or we shall engines find
To move thee, though thou wert a solid rock."

Samson.

Vain were their art if tried; I yield to go.

Exit HARAPHA.

Micah.

So may'st thou act as serves His glory best.

Samson.

Let but that Spirit (which first rushed on me
In the camp of Dan) inspire me at my need:
Then shall I make JEHOVAH's glory known:
Their idol gods shall from His presence fly,
Scattered like sheep before the God of Hosts.

AIR.

Thus when the sun in 's watery bed,
All curtained with a cloudy red,
Pillows his chin upon an orient wave!
The wandering shadows, ghastly pale,
All troop to their infernal jail,
Each fettered ghost slips to his several grave.

[*Exit, led by his Attendant.*

RECITATIVE.

Micah.

With might endued above the sons of men,
Swift as the lightning glance his errand execute,
And spread his name among the heathen round.

AIR AND CHORUS.

Micah and Israelites.

The holy One of Israel be thy guide,
The angel of thy birth stand by thy side:
To fame immortal go,
Heaven bids thee strike the blow:
The Holy One of Israel is thy guide.

RECITATIVE.

Micah.

Old Manoah, with youthful steps, makes haste
To find his son, or bring us some glad news.

Enter MANOAH.

Manoah.

I come, my brethren, not to seek my son,
Who at the feast doth play before the lords;
But give you part with me, what hopes I have
To work his liberty.

AIR AND CHORUS.

Philistines.

Great Dagon has subdued our foe.
And brought their boasted hero low:
Sound out his power in notes divine,
Praise him with mirth, high cheer, and wine.

RECITATIVE.

Manoah.

What noise of joy was that? it tore the sky.

Micah.

They shout and sing to see their dreaded foe
Now captive, blind, delighting with his strength.

Manoah.

Could my inheritance but ransom him,
Without my patrimony, having him,
The richest of my tribe.

Micah.

Sons care to nurse
Their parents in old age; but you, your son.

AIR.

Manoah.

How willing my paternal love
The weight to share
Of filial care,
And part of sorrow's burden prove!
Tho' wandering in the shades of night,
Whilst I have eyes, he wants no light.

RECITATIVE.

Micah.

Your hopes of his delivery seem not vain,
In which all Israel's friends participate.

Manoah.

I know your friendly minds, and—

(*A symphony of horror and confusion.*)

Heaven, what noise?
Horribly loud, unlike the former shout.

CHORUS.

Philistines (*at a little distance*).

Hear us, our god! O hear our cry!
Death! ruin! fallen! no help is nigh:
O mercy, heav'n, we sink, we die!

Enter an ISRAELITISH MESSENGER.

Messenger.

Where shall I run, or which way fly the thoughts
Of this most horrid sight? O countrymen,
You're in this sad event too much concerned.

Micah.

The accident was loud, we long to know from whence.

Messenger.

Let me recover breath; it will burst forth.

Manoah.

Suspense in news is torture: speak it out.

Messenger.

Then take the worst in brief. Samson is dead.

Manoah.

The worst indeed!

Messenger.

Unwounded of his enemies he fell,
At once he did destroy, and was destroyed.
The edifice (where all were met to see)
Upon their heads and on his own he pulled.

Manoah.

O lastly over-strong against thyself!
A dreadful way thou took'st to thy revenge,
Glorious, yet dearly bought.

AIR.

Micah.

Ye sons of Israel, now lament:
Your spear is broke, your bow unbent!
Your glory 's fled;
Amongst the dead
Great Samson lies;
For ever, ever closed his eyes.

CHORUS.

Israelites.

Weep, Israel, weep a louder strain;
Samson, your strength, your hero's slain.

A DEAD MARCH.

Enter ISRAELITES, *with the body of* SAMSON.

SOLI AND CHORUS.

Manoah and Israelites.

Glorious hero, may thy grave
Peace and honour ever have;
After all thy pains and woes,
Rest eternal, sweet repose.

Israelitish Woman.

The virgins, too, shall on their feastful days,
Visit his tomb with flowers, and there bewail
His lot, unfortunate in nuptial choice.

Virgins.

Bring the laurels, bring the bays,
Strew his hearse, and strew the ways.

Israelitish Woman.

May every hero fall like thee,
Thro' sorrow to felicity.

Virgins.

Bring the laurels, bring the bays,
Strew his hearse, and strew the ways.

Israelites.

Glorious hero, may thy grave
Peace and honour ever have;
After all thy pains and woes,
Rest eternal, sweet repose.

RECITATIVE.

Manoah.

Come, come: no time for lamentation now!
No cause for grief; Samson like Samson fell,
Both life and death heroic. To his foes
Ruin is left; to him eternal fame.

AIR.

Israelitish Woman.

Let the bright Seraphim in burning row,
Their loud uplifted Angel-trumpets blow:
Let the Cherubic host, in tuneful choirs,
Touch their immortal harps with golden wires.

CHORUS.

Israelites.

Let their celestial concerts all unite,
Ever to sound His praise in endless morn of light.

PART I.

OVERTURE.

A
tr
f
Ped.
*
mf
cres.

1st time.
2nd time.
p
Adagio.
p
Allegro. ♩= 88.
f
f

p
cres. . . .
f
B
p
cres. . . f

C
p
sf
p
f
Adagio.
ff
MINUET. ♪ = 100.
p

f
tr
mf
tr
tr
cres.
f
Fine.
pp

Dal Segno.

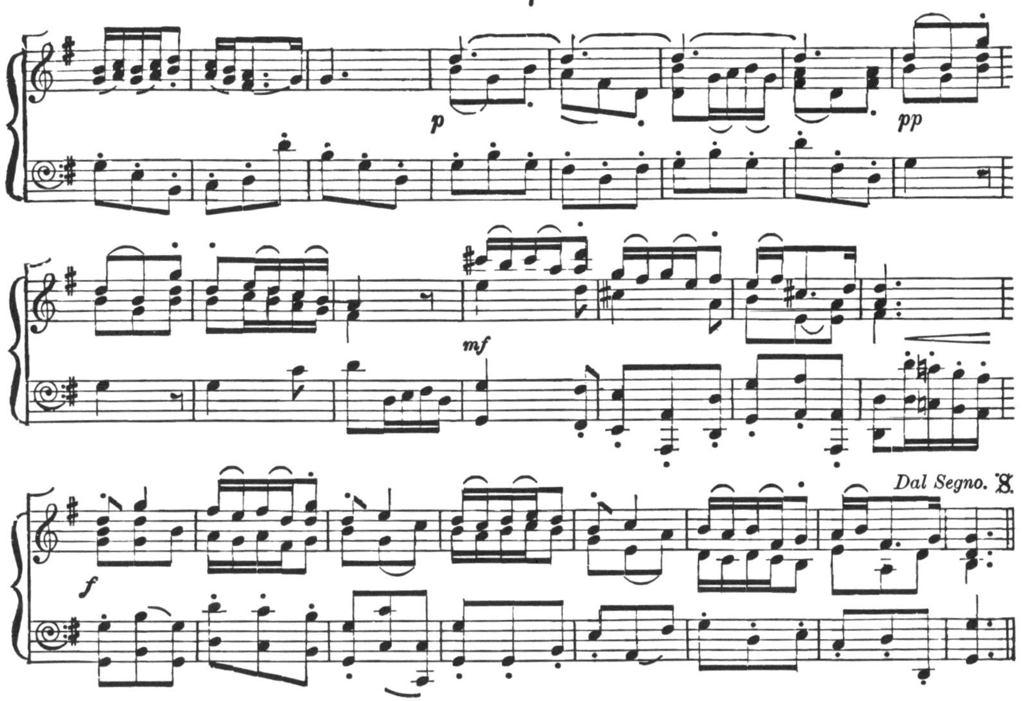

Scene before the Prison in Gaza. SAMSON *blind, and in chains.*

No. 2. RECITATIVE.—"THIS DAY, A SOLEMN FEAST."

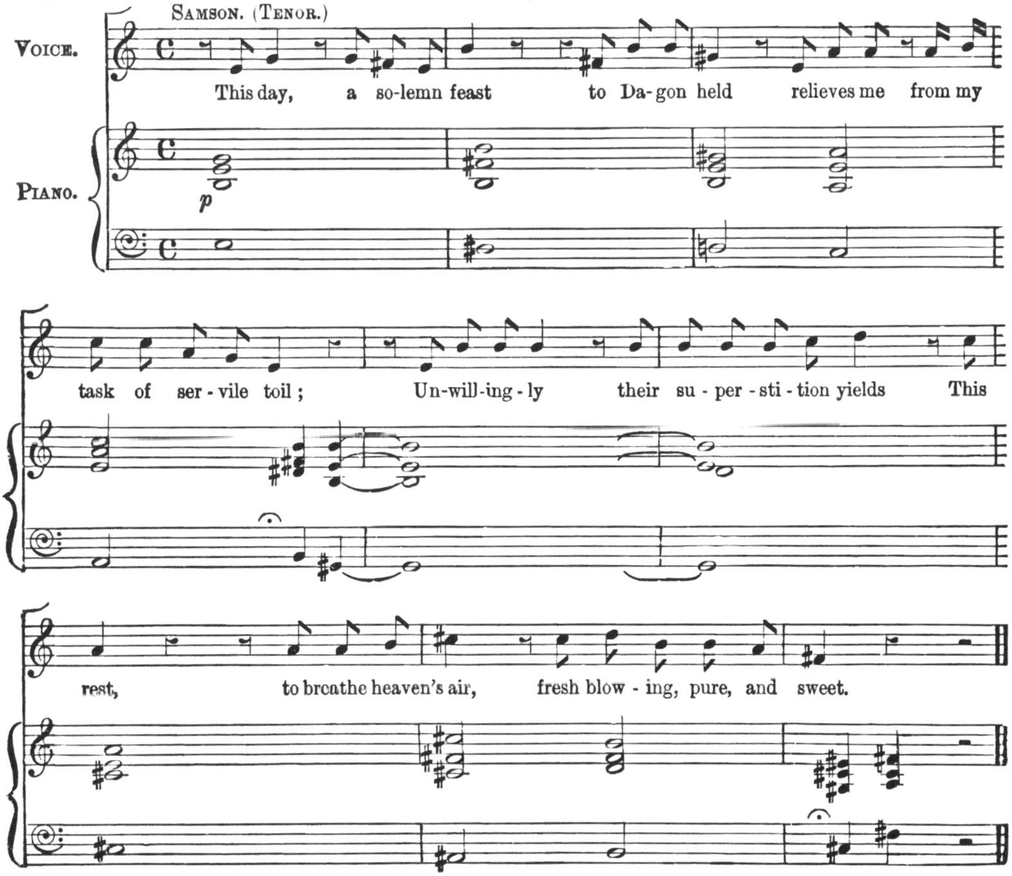
SAMSON. (TENOR.)
VOICE.
PIANO.
This day, a so-lemn feast to Da-gon held relieves me from my
task of ser-vile toil; Un-will-ing-ly their su-per-sti-tion yields This
rest, to breathe heaven's air, fresh blow-ing, pure, and sweet.

Chorus of the Priests of Dagon.

No. 3. "AWAKE THE TRUMPET'S LOFTY SOUND."

A

sound; The joy-ful sa - cred fes - ti - val comes round,

sound; The joy-ful sa - cred fes - ti - val comes round,

sound; The joy-ful sa - cred fes - ti - val comes round,

sound; The joy-ful sa - cred fes - ti - val comes round,

A

ff

When Da - gon king of all the earth, of all the earth is crown'd,

When Da - gon king of all the earth, of all the earth is crown'd,

When Da - gon king of all the earth, of all the earth is crown'd,

When Da - gon king of all the earth, of all the earth is crown'd,

The sa-cred joy - ful, joy - - - - - ful

The sa-cred joy - ful fes - - -

The sa-cred joy - - ful, joy - ful sa-cred

B
A - wake, a-wake, a - wake, The sa-cred joy - ful fes - - - - - ti - val comes round,
fes - ti-val comes round, A-wake, a-wake, The sa-cred joy - ful fes - ti - val comes round,
- - ti-val comes round, A-wake, a-wake, The sa - cred joy - ful fes - - - ti - val comes round,
fes - ti-val comes round, A-wake, a-wake, a - wake, a - wake,
B
f
When Da - gon king of all the earth, of all the earth is crown'd,
When Da - gon king of all the earth, of all the earth is crown'd, when Da - gon
When Da - gon king of all the earth, of all the earth is crown'd, when Da - gon
when Da - gon king, when Da - gon

A-wake the trumpet's loft-y sound,
king . . of all the earth is crown'd, A-wake the trumpet's loft-y sound,
king of all the earth is crown'd, A-wake the trumpet's loft-y
king of all the earth is crown'd, A-wake the
C
The joy-ful sa - cred fes - ti - val comes round,
The joy-ful, joy - ful sa - cred fes - ti - val comes round,
sound, The joy-ful sa - cred fes - ti - val comes round,
trumpet's loft - y sound, The joy-ful sa - cred fes - ti - val comes round,
C
When Da - gon king of all the earth, of all the earth is crown'd,
When Da - gon king of all the earth, of all the earth is crown'd,
When Da - gon king of all the earth, of all the earth is crown'd,
When Da - gon king of all the earth, of all the earth is crown'd,

The sa-cred joy - - - ful fes - - - - - ti-val comes
The sa-cred joy - - - ful fes - - - -
The sa-cred
The sa-cred joy - - - ful, joy - - - ful, sa -
round, the joy-ful fes - tival comes round, A - wake,
- - - - - - - - - - tival comes round, A-wake the trumpet's loft-y
joy - - ful, joy - - ful fes - tival comes round, A-wake the trumpet's loft-y
- cred joy - - ful fes - - - tival comes round, A - wake,
D
D
a-wake the trum - pet's loft - y sound, The joy-ful
sound, a - wake the trum - pet's loft - y sound, The joy-ful
sound, a - wake the trum - pet's loft - y sound, The joy-ful
a - wake the trum - pet's loft - y sound, The joy-ful

sa - cred fes - ti - val comes round, When Da - gon king of all the

sa - cred fes - ti - val comes round, When Da - gon king of all the

sa - cred fes - ti - val comes round, When Da - gon king of all the

sa - cred fes - ti - val comes round, When Da - gon king of all the

earth, of all the earth is crown'd.

earth, . . . of all the earth is crown'd.

earth, of all the earth is crown'd.

earth, of all the earth is crown'd.

No. 4. AIR.—"YE MEN OF GAZA."

Ye men of Ga - za, hith- er bring The mer-ry pipe and pleas-ing string, ye men of
Ga - za, hith - er bring the mer-ry pipe and pleas - ing string,
B
f
p
tr
ye men of Ga - za, hith - er bring the mer-ry
pipe, the mer-ry, mer- ry pipe, ye men of
Ga- za, hith-er bring the mer-ry pipe and pleas-ing string,

C
The so - lemn hymn, and cheer - ful song,
C
p
f
Be Da - gon prais'd by
p
ev' - ry tongue.
D
Ye men of
D
f
p
Ga - za, hith - er bring
The mer-ry, mer - ry
pipe and pleas - ing string,
the mer- ry, mer - ry pipe
and pleas- ing

string, the mer-ry, mer-ry pipe, ... the mer-ry
p
pipe, the mer-ry, mer-ry pipe and pleas - - - - - - - - - - -
tr
tr
tr
- - - - - - - - - - ing string, The
E
E
f
p
so - lemn hymn, and cheer - ful . . song, ... Be
p
Da - gon prais'd by ev' - ry tongue, be Dagon prais'd by ev'- ry tongue, be Da-gon
tr

prais'd by ev' - ry tongue, be Da - gon prais'd,
mf
p
tr
Adagio.
Tempo 1mo.
be Da - gon prais'd by ev' - ry tongue!
Adagio.
Tempo 1mo.
p
f
F
F
tr
tr
tr
mp
tr
tr
f

cut
No. 5. Chorus.—"AWAKE THE TRUMPET'S LOFTY SOUND."
Allegro.
Soprano.
Alto.
Tenor.
Bass.
Piano.
♩= 72.
ff
f
A-wake the trumpet's loft-y sound, The joyful sa - cred fes - ti - val comes round, When Da-gon king of all the earth, of all the earth is crown'd.
A-wake the trumpet's loft-y sound, a-wake the trumpet's loft-y sound, The joy-ful sa - cred fes - ti - val comes round, When Da-gon king of all the earth, . . of all the earth is crown'd.
A-wake the trumpet's loft-y sound, a-wake the trumpet's loft-y sound, The joy-ful sa - cred fes - ti - val comes round, When Da-gon king of all the earth, of all the earth is crown'd.
A-wake the trumpet's loft-y sound, The joy-ful sa - cred fes - ti - val comes round, When Da-gon king of all the earth, of all the earth is crown'd.

Nos. 6, 7 and 8 omitted.

No. 9. Recitative.—"WHY BY AN ANGEL."

Samson.

Voice.

Piano.

p

Why by an An-gel was my birth fore-told, If I must die betray'd, and cap-tiv'd thus, The scorn and gaze of foes; O cru-el thought! My griefs find no re-dress; they in-ward prey, Like gan-gren'd wounds, im-me-di-ca-ble grown.

Nos. 10, 11 and 12 omitted.

No. 13. Recitative.— "MATCHLESS IN MIGHT."

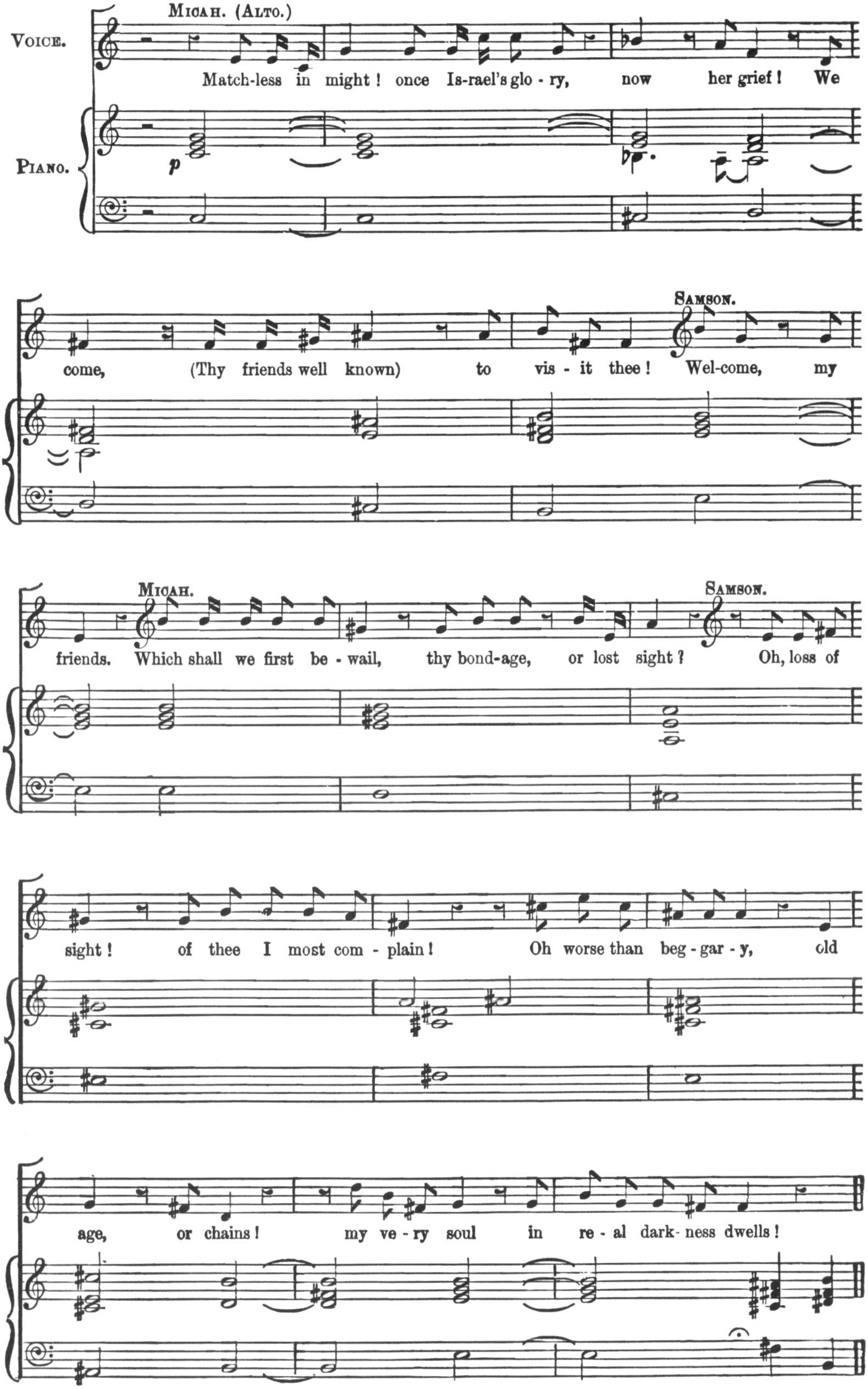
Micah. (Alto.)
Voice.
Piano.
p
Match-less in might! once Is-rael's glo - ry, now her grief! We come, (Thy friends well known) to vis - it thee!
Samson.
Wel-come, my friends.
Micah.
Which shall we first be - wail, thy bond-age, or lost sight?
Samson.
Oh, loss of sight! of thee I most com - plain! Oh worse than beg - gar - y, old age, or chains! my ve - ry soul in re - al dark - ness dwells!

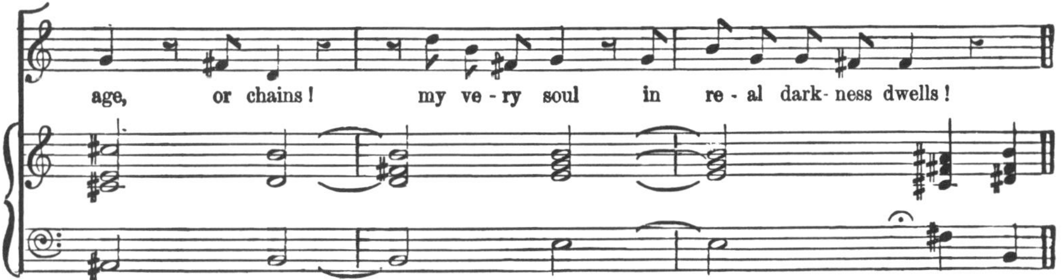

No. 14, AIR.—"TOTAL ECLIPSE."

wel - come day! To - tal e-clipse! no sun, no moon, All

f *p*

dark . . . a-midst the blaze of noon! **B** Why thus de-priv'd Thy

prime de-cree? Sun, moon, and stars are dark to me, sun, moon, and stars,

sun, moon, and stars are dark to me, sun, moon, and stars, sun, moon, and

cres. *pp*

STAND

stars . . are dark to me!

f *p*

No. 15 omitted.

No. 16. CHORUS.—"O FIRST-CREATED BEAM."

and thou, great word, and thou, great word, and
and thou, great word, and thou, great word, Let there be light! and
and thou, great word, and thou, great word, Let there be light! and
Let there be light! and
light was o - ver all, and light, and light was o - ver
light was o - - ver all, and light, and light was o - ver
light was o - - ver all, and light, and light was o - ver
light was o - - ver all, and light, and light was o - - ver
all, and light, and light was o - ver all, o - - ver
all, and light, and light was o - - ver all, o - - ver
all, and light, and light was o - - ver all, o - - ver
all, and light and light was o - - ver all, o - - ver

all, and light was o - - ver all;
all, and light was o - ver all;
all, and light was o - ver all;
all, and light was o - - ver all;
B
One heav'nly blaze shone round this earth-ly ball, shone round this earth-ly ball,
One heav'nly blaze shone round this earth-ly ball, shone round this earth-ly ball,
One heav'nly blaze shone round this earth-ly ball, shone round this earth-ly ball,
One heav'nly blaze shone round this earth-ly ball, shone round this earth-ly ball,
B
To Thy dark ser - vant, to Thy dark ser - vant life by light af - ford,
To
To Thy dark ser - vant, to Thy dark ser - vant life by light af - ford, . . .
To Thy dark
mf

C

life by light af - ford,

Thy dark ser - vant, to Thy dark ser-vant life by light, by light af - ford,

to Thy dark

ser - vant, to Thy dark ser - vant life by light af - ford, by light af - ford, to

C

to Thy dark ser-vant life by light . . af - ford, ...

to Thy dark ser- vant life by light af - ford, life by light af - ford, by light af -

ser - vant, to Thy dark ser - vant, by light, life by light af - ford, by light af -

Thy dark ser - vant, to Thy dark ser - vant life, life by light af - ford, by

. . by light af - ford, to Thy dark ser -vant, to Thy dark

- ford, by light af - ford, to Thy dark ser- vant, to Thy dark

- ford, by light af - ford, to Thy dark ser- vant, to Thy dark ser -vant,

light af - . ford, . . . to Thy dark ser- vant, to Thy dark

f

D
ser - vant life . . . . by light af - ford, . .
ser - vant life . . by light af - ford, to Thy dark ser - vant,
by light, life by light af - ford, to Thy dark ser - vant life by
ser - vant life . . by light af - ford, to Thy dark ser - vant,
D
. . . . . to Thy dark ser - vant life by light, . . by light af -
to Thy dark servant life by light . . af - ford, ... by light af -
light af - ford,
to Thy dark ser - vant, to Thy dark ser - vant life by light, by light af -
- ford, to Thy dark ser - vant life by light af - ford.
- ford, to Thy dark ser - vant life, life by light af - ford.
to Thy dark ser - vant life by light af - ford, life by light . . af - ford.
- ford, to Thy dark ser - vant life by light af - ford.

No. 17 Recitative.—"BRETHREN AND MEN OF DAN."

Nos. 18 and 19 omitted.

No. 20. Recitative.—"THE GOOD WE WISH FOR."

I pray'd for chil-dren, and I gain'd a son, And such a son, as all
men hail'd me hap - py; But who'd be now a fa - ther in my stead? The
bless-ing drew a scorpion's tail be - hind: This plant, se-lect and sa-cred, for a while The
mi - ra - cle of men, was in an hour En-snar'd, as - sault-ed, o-ver-come, led
bound, His foes' de - ri - sion, Cap - tive, poor and blind.
f
p
f
p

No. 21. Air.—"THY GLORIOUS DEEDS."

B
whilst airs of joy . . .
B
cres.
p
. . . . from
thence did flow, ...
cres.
Thy glo-rious deeds, thy glo-rious deeds in - spir'd my tongue, thy
mp
glo - rious deeds in - spir'd my tongue, Whilst airs of joy from thence did flow, . .
p

C
whilst airs of joy
C
cres.
p
from thence did flow,
pp
p
cres.
D
Thy glo - rious deeds in - spir'd my tongue, Whilst airs of joy . . from
D
mp

thence did flow;
f
tr
tr
tr
Largo.
p
To sor - rows now I tune . . . my song, And set my
Largo. ♩= 72.
simile.
p
harp to notes of woe, To sor - rows now I tune my song, And
set . my harp to notes of woe, . . to
E
E

notes of woe, to notes of woe, and set.. my
harp to notes of woe,.. and set my harp to notes.. of
Adagio.
woe. . . . . .
pp
No. 22. Recitative.—"JUSTLY THESE EVILS."
Samson.
Voice.
Just-ly these e-vils have befall'n thy son. Sole author I, sole cause.
Piano.
p
No. 23. Recitative.—"MY GRIEF FOR THIS."
Samson.
Voice.
My grief for this for - bid mine eyes to close, or thoughts to rest:
Piano.
p

But now the strife shall end; me o-ver-thrown, Da-gon pre
-sumes to en-ter lists with God; Who thus pro-vok'd will not con-
-nive, but rouse His fu-ry soon, and His great Name as-
-sert. Da-gon shall stoop, ere long be quite des-
-poil'd Of all those boast-ed tro-phies won on me.
f
p

No. 24. Air.—"WHY DOES THE GOD OF ISRAEL SLEEP."

- rise with dread-ful sound, a - rise with dreadful sound, ... with dreadful
B
sound, a - rise, a - rise with dread - ful sound, with
B
f
p
dread - ful sound, a - rise, a - rise, a -
f
p
- rise with dreadful sound, with dreadful sound, With clouds encompass'd round. . .
p
. . . with clouds encompass'd round, ...
tr
tr

Then shall the hea-then hear Thy
tr
thun - - der, then shall the heath-en hear Thy thun - - - - - - -
- - der, . . Thy thun - der deep.
The
D
tem - pest of Thy wrath now raise, In
f
mp
f

whirlwinds them pur-sue, Full fraught with vengeance due, in whirlwinds them pursue, . . .
p
sf
p
. . . . in whirlwinds them pursue, them pur - sue, them pur-sue, Full
fraught with ven-geance due, full fraught with ven - - - - - - - - - - - -
- - - - - geance due,
E
Till
f
f
tr
p
shame and trou-ble all . . . .
sf

. . thy foes shall seize,
till
shame,
till shame and
trou - ble,
till shame and
trou - ble
all
thy foes shall
seize,
till shame and
trou - ble
all . . . .
thy foes shall
seize, ...
. . . .
till
shame
and trou - ble

all . . . . thy foes . . .
. . . . . shall seize.
F
F
f
Why does the God of Is-rael sleep?
p
A-rise with dread-ful sound, a-rise, a-rise, a-
f
p
-rise with dreadful sound, With clouds encompass'd round, ... encompass'd

G
round, Then shall the heathen hear Thy thun - - der deep. The
G
f
p
tem - pest of Thy wrath now raise, In whirl - winds them pur -
mf
p
- - sue, them pur-sue, Full fraught with ven - - - - - -
tr
tr
mf
p
- - - - - - geance due,
H
Till
H
tr
f
p
shame and trou-ble, till shame and
tr
tr
tr
tr
tr
tr

No. 25 OMITTED.

No. 26. CHORUS.—"THEN SHALL THEY KNOW."

shall they know that He, whose Name . . . . Je -
Then shall they know that He, whose
Then shall they know that He, . . whose Name, that He whose
know that He, whose Name . . . Je -
B
- ho - vah, is a - lone O'er all the earth, but One,
Name Je - ho - vah, is a - lone O'er all the earth, but One,
Name Je - ho - vah, is a - lone O'er all the earth, but One, Was
- ho - vah, is a - lone O'er all . . . the earth, but One,
B
f
Was ev - er the Most
ev - er the Most High, and still the same, and still the same, . . .

Was ev - er the Most
High, . . and still the same, and still the same, . . .
. . . . and still the same, . . .
High, . . and still the same, and still the same,
. . . . and still the same,
and still the same, and still the same, . .
Was ev - er the Most
f
C
was ev - er the Most
was ev - er the Most
. . . . and still the same, . . . and still the
High, . . and still the same, and still the same, . . . ,
C

High, . . and still the same, and still the same, . .
High, and still, and still the same, . . was ev - er
same, and . . still, and still the same, . . was ev - er . .
. . . . and still the same, was ev - er the Most
. . . . and still the same. Then shall they know that He, whose Name Je -
the Most High, and still the same. Then shall they know that He, whose Name Je - ho -
the Most High, and still the same. Then shall they know that He, whose Name Je -
High, and still the same. . . Then shall they know that He, whose Name Je -
D
- ho-vah, is a - lone O'er all the earth, but One, Was
- vah, is a - lone O'er all the earth, but One, and still the same,
- ho-vah, is a - lone . . O'er all the earth, but One, and still the same, . .
- ho-vah, is a - lone . . O'er all the earth, but One,
D

ev - er the Most High, was ev - er the Most
Was ev - er the Most High, . . . and still the same,
. . . and still the same, was ev - er the Most
and still the same, . . . and still the same, . . .
High, . . and still the same, Je - ho - vah is a - lone o'er
and still the same, and still the same, Je - ho - vah is a - lone o'er
High, . . . and still the same, Je - ho - vah is a - lone o'er
. . . . and still the same, Je - ho - vah is a - lone o'er
E
E
all the earth, but One, and still the same, ... and still
all the earth, but One, was ev - er the Most High, and still, and
all the earth, but One, was ev - er the . . Most High, . . . and
all the earth, but One, was ev - er the Most High, . . and

. . . the same, was ev - er the Most High, and still the same.
still the same, was ev - er the Most High, and still the same.
still the same, was ev - er the Most High, and still the same.
still the same, was ev - er the Most High, and still the same.
ff
No. 27. Recitative.—" FOR THEE, MY DEAREST SON."
Manoah.
Voice.
For thee, my dear - est son— must thou mean - while
Piano.
p
Lie, thus neg- lect - ed, in this loath-some plight.
Samson.
It should be so.
Why should I live? Soon shall these orbs to dou - ble dark- ness yield.

No. 28.

Recitative.—"MY GENIAL SPIRITS DROOP."

Nos. 29 and 30 omitted.

No. 31. Chorus.—" THEN ROUND ABOUT THE STARRY THRONE."
A tempo ordinario.
Soprano.
Then round a - bout the star - ry throne . . . Of Him who
Alto.
Then round a - bout the star - ry throne . . . Of Him who
Tenor.
Then round a - bout the star - ry throne . . . Of Him who
Bass.
Then round a - bout the star - ry throne . . . Of Him who
A tempo ordinario.
Piano.
♩ = 76.
ev - er . . rules a - lone,
Your
ev - er rules a - lone,
Your heav'n - ly
ev - er rules a - lone,
Your heav'n -
ev - er rules a - lone,
A
heav'n - ly guid - ed soul shall climb, your heav'n - ly guid - ed soul shall
guid - - - - ed soul, . . your heav'n - ly guid - - - - ed
- ly guid - - - ed soul, . . your heav'n - ly guid - - - -
your heav'n - ly guid - ed soul, . . your heav'nly guid - -

B
climb, your heav'nly guid - ed soul shall climb; Of all this earthly
soul, . . your heav'nly guid-ed soul shall climb; Of all this earthly
- - - - - - - - - ed soul shall climb; Of all this earthly
- - - - - - - - - ed soul shall climb; Of all this earthly
B
gross - ness quit, With glo - ry crown'd . .
gross - ness quit, With glo - ry crown'd . .
gross - ness quit, With glo -
gross - ness quit, With glo - ry
C
. . . . for ev - er sit,
. . . . for ev - er sit, And
- ry crown'd for ev - er, for ev - er sit, And triumph o-ver Death, and thee, O Time, and
crown'd . . . . . for ev - er sit,
C

and triumph o-ver Death, and

triumph over Death, and thee, O Time, and thee, O Time, . . . and thee, O Time, and thee,

tri - - umph o-ver Death, and thee, O Time, . . . and thee, O . . Time, and

and triumph over Death, and thee, O Time, and

D

thee, O Time! With glo - ry crown'd, .

. . . O Time! With glo - ry crown'd, ... with glo - ry

thee, O Time! With glo - ry crown'd, ... with glo - ry crown'd, . .

thee, O Time! With glo - ry crown'd, ... with glo - ry

E

. . . . . for ev - - er, for ev - er sit, and

crown'd, . . with glo - ry crown'd, for ev - er sit,

. . . . . with glo - ry crown'd, for ev - er sit, and triumph o-ver Death, and

crown'd, ... for ev - er sit, for ev - - - -

END OF FIRST PART

PART II.

Nos. 32 and 33 omitted.

God . . of Hosts, O God, re - turn, O God of Hosts! be -
- hold, be-hold Thy ser - vant in dis - tress, . . . be - hold Thy
ser-vant in dis - tress, Re-turn, O . . God! be - hold . . . Thy ser -
- vant in dis-tress, re - turn, O God, re -
B
B
f
p
pp
- turn, O God of Hosts! be-hold, be - hold, be - hold, be-hold Thy ser-vant, Thy
p
f
p

C
ser - vant in distress, be-hold, be-hold Thy ser-vant, Thy ser-vant in dis -
C
f
- tress, ... re-turn, re - turn, O God, re-turn, O God of
sf
p
STAND
Hosts! be-hold, be - hold Thy ser - vant in . . dis-tress,
f
Fine.
to p. 60
tr
Fine.
p
CUT
D
His migh - ty griefs, his migh-ty griefs re-dress, his migh-ty
D
pp

griefs, his mighty griefs, his mighty griefs redress,
Nor by the heathen be they told, nor by the heathen be they told,
His mighty griefs . . . . re - dress, Nor by the
heathen, by the hea- then be they told, nor by the hea - then be . . they told.
D.C.
D.C.

No. 36. CHORUS.—"TO DUST HIS GLORY THEY WOULD TREAD."

Largo.

SOLO.

SOPRANO.

To dust his glo-ry they would tread, And num-ber him amongst the dead,

ALTO.

To dust his glo-ry they would tread, And num-ber him amongst the dead, and

TENOR.

To dust his glo-ry they would tread, And num-ber him amongst the dead,

BASS.

To dust his glo-ry they would tread, And num-ber him amongst the dead,

Largo.

PIANO. ♪ = 69.

amongst the dead, . . . a - mongst the

num-ber him amongst the dead, and num-ber him a-mongst the

and num - ber him, and num-ber him a-mongst the

and num-ber him a-mongst the

A
MICAH.
Re -
dead, and num - ber him amongst the dead.
dead, and num - ber him amongst the dead.
dead, and num - ber him amongst the dead.
dead, and num - ber him amongst the dead.
dim.
p
pp
p
- turn, re-turn, O God of Hosts! be - hold, be-hold Thy ser-vant in dis-tress, be -
B
To dust his
To dust his
To dust his
To dust his
f

hold,
be-hold, O God of Hosts,
glo-ry they would tread,
And number him a-mongst the
glo-ry they would tread,
And number him a-mongst the
glo-ry they would tread,
And num-ber him a-mongst the
glo-ry they would tread,
And num-ber him a-mongst the
mf
be-hold Thy servant, Thy ser-vant in dis-tress, O God, be-hold!
dead,
and num-ber him a-mongst the dead.
dead,
and num-ber him a-mongst the dead.
dead,
and num-ber him a-mongst the dead.
dead,
and num-ber him a-mongst the dead.
p

To dust his glo - ry they would tread, to dust his glo - ry they would tread, And num - ber
him a-mongst the dead.
C
To dust his glo -ry they would tread, And num - ber
To dust his glo -ry they would tread, And num - ber
To dust his glo - ry they would tread, And num - ber
To dust his glo - ry they would tread, And num - ber
C
pp
f

him amongst the dead, and number him amongst the dead, and
him amongst the dead, and number him amongst the dead, and
him amongst the dead, and number him amongst the dead, and
him amongst the dead, and number him amongst the dead, and
p
pp
num - ber him a - mongst the dead.
num - ber him a - mongst the dead.
num - ber him a - mongst the dead.
num - ber him a - mongst the dead.
f
tr
p
pp

No. 37.
Recitative.—"BUT WHO IS THIS?"
Voice.
Piano.
Micah.
But who is this, that so be-deck'd and gay, Comes this way sail-ing like a state-ly ship? 'Tis Da-li-la, thy wife.
Samson.
My wife, my trait-ress! let her not come near me.
Dalila.
With doubtful feet, and wav'ring re-so-lu-tion, I come, O Samson, dread-ing thy dis-plea-sure; But con-ju-gal af-fec-tion led me on, Pre-vail-ing o-ver fear and tim'-rous doubt. Glad if in aught my help or love could serve to ex-pi-ate my rash, un-thought mis-deed.
p

No. 38. AIR.—"WITH PLAINTIVE NOTES."

With plain - tive notes and
am' - rous moan, with plain - tive notes, and am' - rous moan,
Thus, . . thus, thus coos . . . . the tur-tle left a-lone, thus
coos, thus coos the tur - tle left a - lone, ... thus
coos, . . . thus coos . . . . the tur - tle left a - lone.
tr
f

B
B
tr
mf
With plain - tive notes and am' - rous moan, Thus
p
coos . . the tur-tle, thus coos, thus coos the
tur-tle left a-lone, thus,. . thus, thus coos . . . . the
tur - - - tle, thus coos, ... thus
C
C

Nos. 39 to 42 omitted

No. 43. Solo.—" MY FAITH AND TRUTH."

B

but hear me, hear me, hear.. me, hear the

voice of.. love. My faith..and truth, O Sam - son,

f *p*

C

prove, But hear me, hear me,

tr

pp

hear me, but hear me,.. hear the voice of love.

f

D

With love no mor - tal can.. be

p

F

E
cloy'd, All hap - pi - ness is love en - joy'd,
all hap - pi -
E
tr
mf
p
- ness is love en - joy'd,
With love no mor - tal can be
tr
mf
p
cloy'd,
All hap - pi - ness, all hap - pi - ness is
mf
p
love en - joy'd.
F
My faith . . and
F
f
truth, O Sam - son, prove, . . But hear . . me, hear the voice of

No. 44. CHORUS OF VIRGINS.—"HER FAITH AND TRUTH."

H

mf

Her faith and . . truth, O Sam - son,

faith and . . truth, O Sam - son, prove,

H

prove, But hear . . . her, hear . . . .

p

But hear . . . . me, hear . . . . the

the voice of love, but hear . . .

voice of love but hear . . . . the

p

. . . the voice of . . . love, hear her.

voice of . . . love, but hear me.

I

Her faith and . . truth, O . . Sam-son, . . prove, But hear her, . .

My faith and . . truth, O . . Sam-son, . . prove, But hear me, . .

hear . . . . the voice of love!

hear . . . . the voice of love!

Nos. 45 to 49 omitted.

No. 50. Recitative.—"NE'ER THINK OF THAT."

Samson.

Voice.

Piano.

Ne'er think of that, I know thy warb-ling charms, Thy trains, thy wiles, and fair en-chant-ed cup. Their force is null'd. Where once I have been caught, I shun the snare. These chains, this pri-son-house, I count the house of li-ber-ty to thine.

No. 51. DUET.—"TRAITOR TO LOVE!"

B
threats give o'er.
Samson.
Trait - ress to love, I'll hear no.. more.
B
p
The charmer's voice, your arts give o'er, the charmer's voice, . . your
C
Trait - or to love, trait - or to
arts give o'er!
Trait - ress to love,
C
love, I'll sue no more, I'll sue no more For par-don
trait - ress to love, I'll hear no more the charmer's voice,

scorn'd, your threats give o'er, your threats give
your arts give o'er, give o - ver your arts,
o'er, I'll sue no more, I'll sue . . no more, I'll sue no more,
I'll hear no more, no more, I'll hear . . no more, I'll hear no
D
your threats give o'er, Trait - or to love trait - or to love! I'll
more, I'll hear no more! Trait - ress to love, trait - ress to
D
mf
sue no . . more For par - don scorn'd, I'll sue . . no more, no
love! I'll hear no . . more, The charm - er's voice, the charm - -

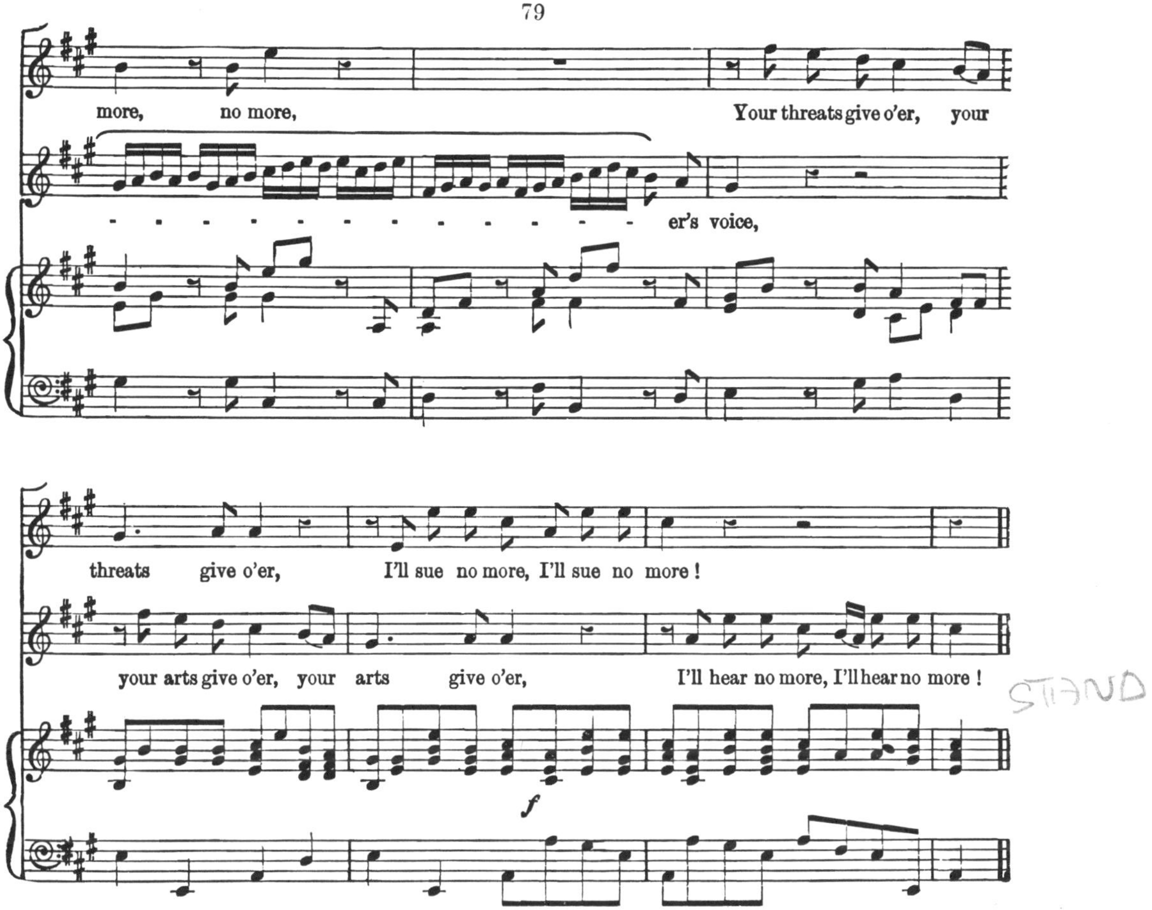
more, no more, Your threats give o'er, your
- - - - - - - - - - - - - - er's voice,
threats give o'er, I'll sue no more, I'll sue no more!
your arts give o'er, your arts give o'er, I'll hear no more, I'll hear no more!
f
STAND

Nos. 52 and 53 omitted.

No. 54. Recitative.—"FAVOUR'D OF HEAVEN."

Samson.
Voice.
Piano.
Fa - vour'd of heaven is he who finds one
p
true; How rare - ly found!— his way to peace is smooth.

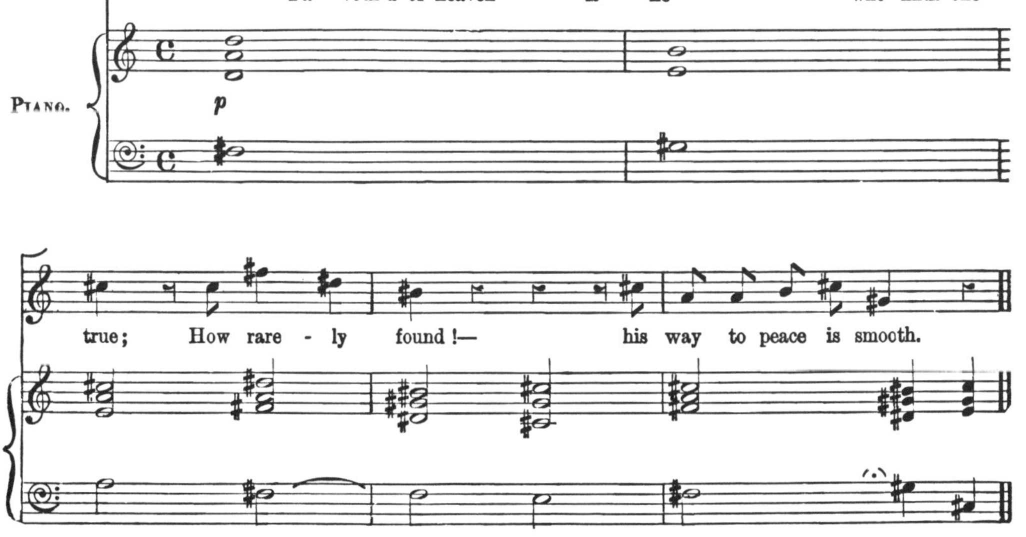

No. 55. CHORUS.—"TO MAN GOD'S UNIVERSAL LAW."

Grave.

SOPRANO. To man God's u-ni-ver-sal law

ALTO. To man God's u-ni-ver-sal law, to man, to man God's u-ni-ver-sal law

TENOR. To man God's u-ni-ver-sal law, to man God's u-ni-ver-sal law

BASS. To man God's u-ni-ver-sal, u-ni-ver-sal law

PIANO. ♩= 66.

Gave pow'r to keep his wife in awe, gave pow'r to keep his wife in awe;

Gave pow'r to keep his wife in awe;

Gave pow'r to keep his wife in awe, gave pow'r to keep his wife in awe;

Gave pow'r, gave pow'r to keep his wife in awe;

Allegro moderato.

Thus shall his life be ne'er dis-may'd, By fe-male u-sur-pa-tion

Thus shall his life be ne'er dis-may'd,

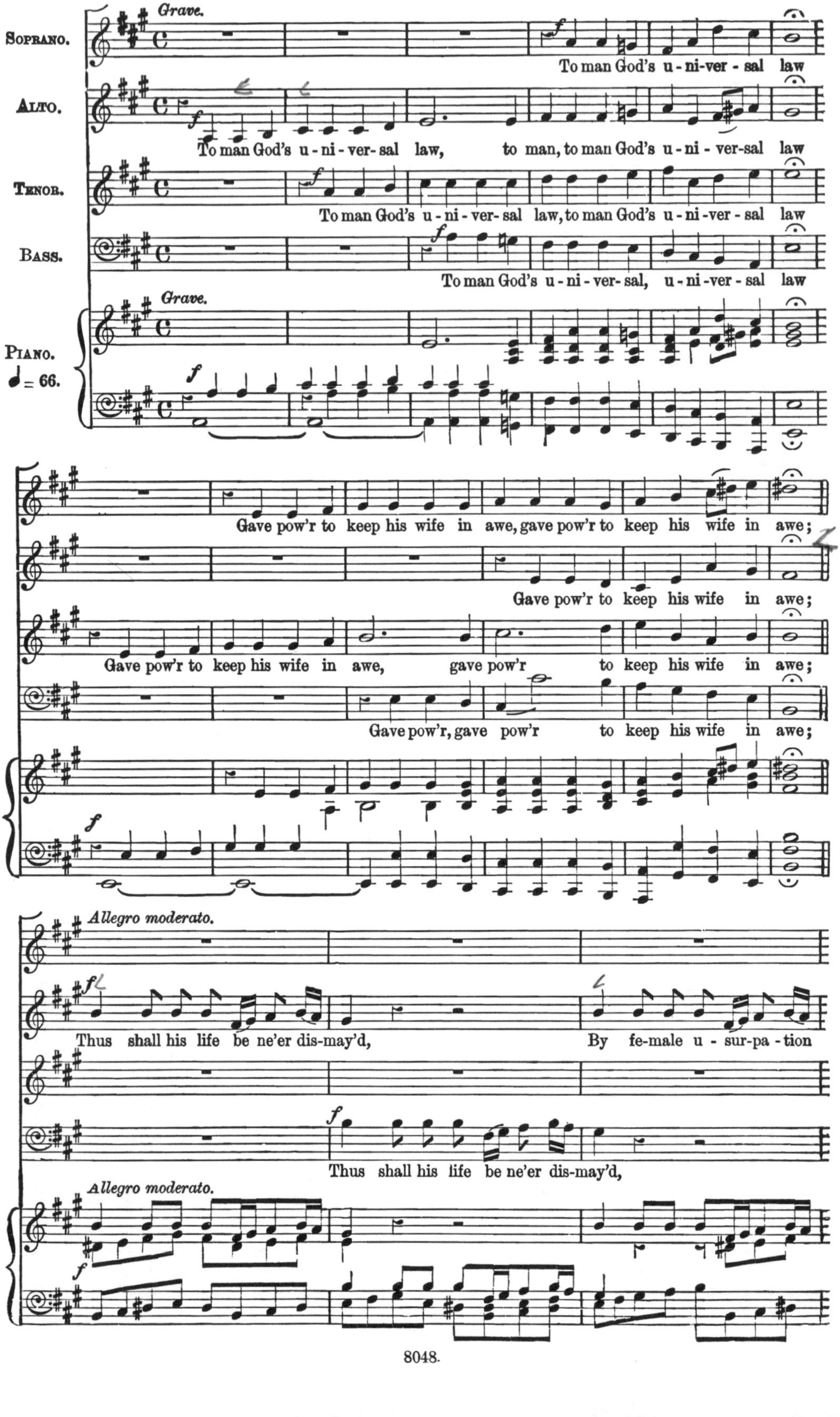

Thus shall his life be ne'er dis-
sway'd,
Thus shall his life be ne'er dis-may'd,
By female u-sur-pa-tion sway'd,
-may'd,
By fe-male u-sur-pa-tion sway'd,
By fe-male u-sur-pa-tion
By fe-male u-sur-pa-tion sway'd,
A
by fe-male u-sur-pa
sway'd,
Thus shall his life be ne'er dis-may'd,
Thus shall his life be ne'er dis-may'd,
A

tion sway'd, . .
sway'd, ...
by fe-male u - sur - pa-tion sway'd,
sway'd, ...
by fe-male u - sur - pa - tion sway'd, . .
by fe-male u - sur - pa -
by fe-male u - sur-pa- tion sway'd, ...
. . .
sway'd, . .
thus shall his life be ne'er dis - may'd, ...
by female u-sur-pa-tion,
- - - - - tion sway'd, . .
by female u-sur -
thus shall his life . . . be ne'er dis- may'd, . .
B
by female u-sur-pa-tion sway'd,
by female u - sur- pa - - -
thus shall his life be ne'er dis-may'd,
by female u-sur -
- pa - - - tion sway'd, by fe-male u-sur - pa - - tion sway'd, thus
by female u - sur - pa - - - tion sway'd,
thus
B

tion sway'd, by female u-sur-
pa - tion sway'd,
shall his life be ne'er dis - may'd, dis - may'd, By
shall his life be ne'er dis-may'd, By fe-male u - sur - pa
pa - tion sway'd, sway'd,
C
Thus shall his life be ne'er dis-
Thus shall his life be ne'er dis-may'd, By fe - male u - sur - pa - tion
fe-male u - sur - pa - tion sway'd,
tion sway'd,
may'd, sway'd, By
sway'd, By fe-male u- sur-
Thus shall his life be ne'er dis - may'd, dis - may'd, By female u - sur -
Thus shall his life be ne'er dis -

fe-male u-sur-pa - - - tior sway'd,
pa-tion sway'd, sway'd, by fe-male u-sur-pa - tion
pa - - - tion sway'd,
may'd, By fe - male u - sur-pa - - - tion sway'd,
D
by female u-sur-pa-tion, by female u-sur-pa-tion sway'd,
sway'd, by female u-sur-pa-tion sway'd, sway'd,
by female u-sur-pa-tion, by female u-sur-pa-tion sway'd,
by female u-sur-pa-tion sway'd,
D
Andante.
Thus shall his life be ne'er dis-may'd, By fe-male u-sur-pa - tion sway'd.
Thus shall his life be ne'er dis-may'd, By fe-male u-sur-pa - tion sway'd.
Thus shall his life be ne'er dis-may'd, By fe-male u-sur-pa - tion sway'd.
Thus shall his life be ne'er dis-may'd, By fe-male u-sur-pa - tion sway'd.
Andante.

No. 56. RECITATIVE.—"NO WORDS OF PEACE."

SAMSON.
HARAPHA.
- pearance answers loud re - port. The way to know, were not to see, but taste. Ha ! dost thou
then al - rea - dy sin - gle me ? I thought that la - bour and thy chains had
tam'd thee. Had fortune brought me to that field of death, Where thou wrought'st wonders with an ass -'s
SAMSON.
jaw, I'd left thy car-case where the ass lay dead. Boast not of what thou wouldst have done, but
HARAPHA.
do. The hon - our cer - tain to have won from thee I lose, pre -
- vent - ed by thy eyes put out ; To com - bat with a blind man I dis - dain.

No. 57.

Air.—"HONOUR AND ARMS."

Allegro.

Voice.

Allegro.

Piano.

♩ = 92.

f

A

Harapha.

𝄋 A

p

Hon-our and arms . . . . scorn such a foe, scorn such . a foe,

cres.

p

Though I could end thee at a blow,

G

though I could end thee at a blow, though I could end thee at a blow,

p

Poor vic - to - ry, to con - quer thee, Or

glo - - - - - - - - - - - - - - ry in . . thy

o - ver-throw!

B

f

Hon - our and arms . . . . . scorn such a foe, scorn

p

such a foe, Though I could end thee at a blow, though I could
p
end thee at a blow, Poor vic - to - ry, to con - quer thee, poor vic- to- ry,
to con - quer thee, Or glo - - - - - ry, or glo -
- - - - - - - - - ry in thy o - ver- throw, or
C
mf
glo - ry, or glo - ry, or glo - - - -
p

- - - - - - - - - - - ry in thy o - ver - throw!
f
Fine.
Fine.
Van - quish a slave that is half slain! So mean a tri - umph I dis-dain, so
p
mean a tri - umph I dis - dain, ... I dis-dain,

Nos. 58 and 59 omitted.

No. 60. RECITATIVE.—"CAM'ST THOU FOR THIS."

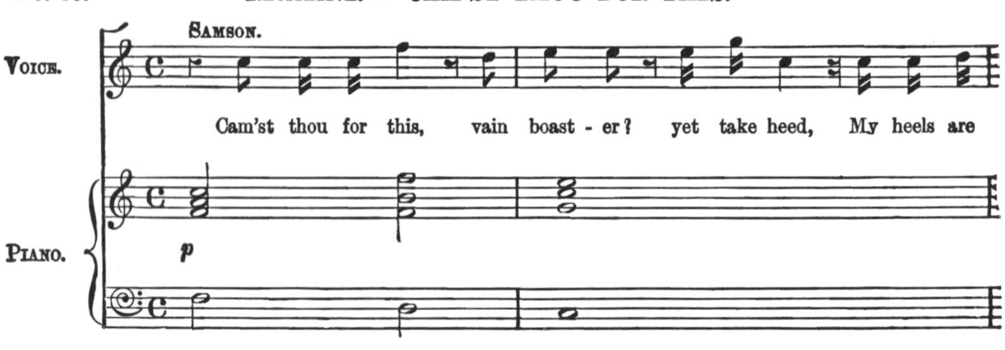

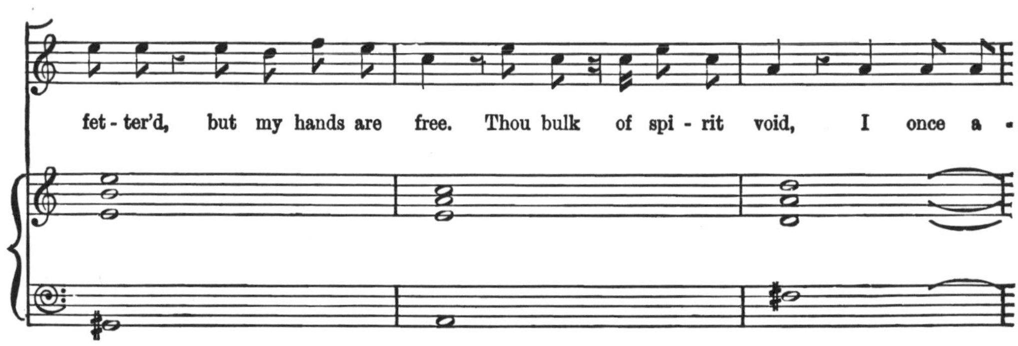

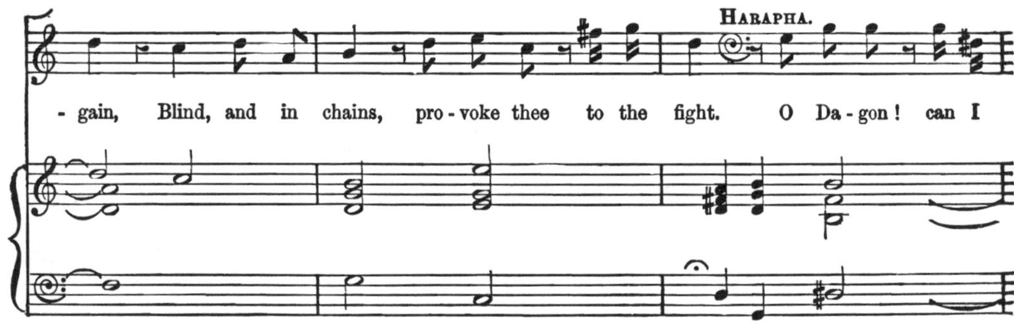

No. 61. DUET.—"GO, BAFFLED COWARD, GO."

speed, fly, Go, go, baf-fled, cow-ard, baf-fled cow-ard, baf-fled
cow-ard, go, baf - fled cow-ard, go, Lest vengeance lay thee low; In safe- ty fly my
wrath, ... fly, fly my wrath with
B
speed.
B
f

Harapha.
Presume not on thy God, pre-sume not on thy God, Who un-der foot has
trod, who un-der foot has trod Thy strength and thee, thy strength and
thee, at great - est need, who un-der foot has trod thy strength and
thee, at great - est need. Presume not on thy God, presume not on thy
C
Go, baf-fled cow-ard, go, go, baf-fled cow-ard, go, go,
p

baf - fled cow-ard go, go, baf- fled cow-ard, baf-fled cow-ard, baf -fled cow-ard, go, baf-fled cow-ard,
God, presume not, pre-sume not, presume not, pre-sume not on thy God, on thy
go, Lest vengeance lay thee low, ... go, fly,
God, Who un - der foot has trod thy strength and thee, at
in safe- ty fly my wrath, ...
great - - est need, Presume not,
D
. . go, baf - fled cow-ard, go, go, baf-fled cow-ard, baf-fled cow-ard, baf-fled
presume not, pre-sume not on thy God, pre-sume not, pre-sume not, pre
D

cow-ard go, in safe - ty fly my wrath, ...
-sume not on thy God, Who un-der foot has trod thy strength and thee, at
. . go, fly my wrath with speed, go, fly, go, baf-fled
great-est, greatest need, at greatest, great - - - - est need.
E
cow-ard, baf-fled cow-ard, in safe - ty fly . . my wrath with speed.
E
f

STAND

No. 62. RECITATIVE.—"HERE LIES THE PROOF."

No. 63. CHORUS.—"HEAR, JACOB'S GOD."

Save . . us, save us,
Is - rael depends on
Save us, save . . us,
Is - rael depends on
Save . . us, save us, save . . . .
Save us, save . . . . . . us, and
Save us, save . . .
Thee a-lone;
Save . . . us, save us, and
Thee a - lone, . . . on Thee a - lone,
Thee a - lone, . . . on Thee a - lone, save . . .
us, Is - rael de-pends on Thee a - lone, save . . . . .
show that Thou art near, that Thou art near, . . . Is - rael de-pends on
us, Is - rael depends on
show that Thou art near, that Thou art near, that Thou . . . art

B

Is - rael depends on Thee a - lone, save . . us, and show . .

us, and show that Thou art near, save . . us, and show . .

us, and show that Thou art near, save . . us, save us, and

Thee a - lone, on Thee, save . . us, save . . us, and

Thee a - lone, on Thee, save . . us, and show that

near, and show that Thou art near, save . . us, and

B

. . that Thou art near! O Ja - cob's God, Je - ho - vah, hear!

. . that Thou art near! O . . . Ja - cob's God, Je - ho - vah, hear!

show that Thou art near! O Ja - cob's God, Je - ho - vah, hear!

show that Thou art near! O . . . Ja - cob's God, Je - ho - vah, hear!

Thou art near! O Ja - cob's God, Je - ho - vah, hear!

show that Thou art near! O Ja - cob's God, Je - ho - vah, hear!

f
C
O save us, prostrate at Thy throne! Israel depends on Thee alone;
O save us, pros-trate at Thy throne! Is - rael de-pends on Thee a -
O save us, pros·trate at Thy throne! Is - rael de-pends on Thee a
O save us, pros-trate at Thy throne! Is rael de-pends on Thee a -
O save us, pros-trate at Thy throne! Is - rael de-pends on Thee a -
O save us, pros-trate at Thy throne! Is - rael de-pends on Thee a -
O save us, pros-trate at Thy throne! Is - rael de-pends on Thee a -
C
- lone; Save . . us, save . . us, Is - rael depends on
- lone; Save . . us, save . . . . .
- lone; Save us, save . . us,
- lone; Save . . us, save . . us, save . . . us, and
- lone; Save us, save us,
- lone; Save us, save us, save us, and show that Thou art near, that Thou art

Thee a-lone, save . . us, save us, save . . us, save
. . . us, save . . us, save . . us, and
Is-rael de-pends on Thee a-lone, on Thee, on Thee a-lone, save . . us, and
show that Thou art near, Is-rael depends on Thee, save . . us, and
Is-rael depends on Thee a-lone,
near, save . . us, save us, and show that Thou art
. . . us, and show that Thou art near, that Thou . . art near.
show that Thou art near, that Thou art near, that Thou . . art near.
show that Thou art near, that Thou art near, that Thou . . art near.
show that Thou art near, that Thou art near, that Thou . . art near.
save us, and show that Thou art near, that Thou . . art near.
near, and show that Thou art near, that Thou . . art near.

H

No. 64. RECITATIVE.—"DAGON, ARISE!"

No. 65 OMITTED.

No. 66. CHORUS.—"TO SONG AND DANCE."

Allegro.

SOPRANO.

ALTO.

TENOR.

BASS.

Allegro.

PIANO.
♩ = 76.

mf

f

f
To song and dance, ... to song and dance, ...

f
To song and dance, . . .

. . To song and dance we give the day,
to song and dance we give the
To song and dance we give the day,
to song and dance we give the
. . To song and dance we give the day,
to song and dance we give the
To song and dance we give the day
to song and dance we give the
day, ... we give the day,
Which shows Thy u - ni - ver - sal
day, we give the day,
Which shows Thy u - ni - ver - sal
day we give the day,
Which shows Thy u - ni - ver - sal
day, we give the day,
Which shows Thy u - ni - ver - sal
A
A
sway, Thy u - ni - ver - - - - - - - - - - -
sway, Thy u - ni - ver - sal sway, which
sway, Thy u - ni - ver - sal sway, which
sway, Thy u - ni - ver - sal sway, which

- - - - - - sal sway, which shows . . . Thy u-ni-ver-sal
shows Thy u-ni-ver-sal sway, which shows . . . . .
shows Thy u-ni-ver-sal sway, Thy u-ni-ver-sal sway, Thy u-ni-ver-sal
shows . . . . Thy u-ni-ver-sal
sway, which shows, which shows Thy u-ni-ver-sal
. . . . Thy u-ni-ver-sal
sway, which shows, which shows Thy u-ni-ver-sal
sway, which shows, which shows Thy u-ni-ver-sal
B
sway. To song and dance, . . . and
sway. To song and dance, . . . and
sway. To song and dance, . . . to dance and
sway. to dance and
B

song,
to dance and song . . . we give the
song, to dance and song . . . . we give . . . the
song,
song,
to dance and
day, to dance and song . . . we give the day, which shows Thy
day, to song and dance, to song and dance we give the day, which shows Thy
to dance and song . . . we give the day, which shows Thy
song . . . . we give the day, which shows Thy
C
u - - ni - ver - - sal sway.
u - - ni - ver - - - sal sway.
u - - ni - ver - - - sal sway.
u - ni - ver - sal sway.
C

Pro - tect us by Thy might - y hand, pro - tect us,
Pro - tect us by Thy might - y hand,
Pro - tect us by Thy might - y hand,
Pro - tect us by Thy might - y hand, pro-tect us,
pro-tect us, pro - tect us, pro-tect us by Thy
pro - tect us, pro-tect us, pro - tect us, pro-tect us by Thy
pro-tect us, pro-tect us, pro - tect us, pro-tect us by Thy
pro-tect us, pro - tect us, pro-tect us by Thy
D
might - y hand, And sweep this race . . . . from out . . . the
might - y hand, And sweep this race . . . from out the
might - y hand, And sweep this
might - y hand,
D

land, and sweep this race, this race from out the land, and sweep this
land, and sweep this race, this race from out the land, and sweep this
race, ... this race from out the land, and sweep this
and sweep this race . . . . from out the land, and sweep this
race from out the land.
race from out the land.
race from out the land.
race from out . . . the land.

No. 67. CHORUS.—"FIX'D IN HIS EVERLASTING SEAT."

Great Da - gon rules the world, ...

Je - ho - vah,

Je - ho - vah,

MANOAH. HARAPHA.

Je - ho - vah, Great Da - gon,

. . . . rules the world, rules the world in state,

B

rules the world, . . . rules the world in state, Je -

rules the world, rules the world in state, Je

CHORUS. MANOAH.

rules the world . . . . in state, Je -

B

Great Da - gon, great Da - gon

- ho - vah, Je - ho - vah

- ho - vah, Je - ho - vah

HARAPHA. MANOAH. HARAPHA.

- ho - vah, Great Da - gon, Je - ho - vah Great Da - gon

C

rules the world in state, Great

rules the world in state, Je - ho - vah,

rules the world in state, Je - ho - vah,

CHORUS. MANOAH. HARAPHA.

rules the world in state, Je - ho - vah, Great

C

Da - gon, Great Da - gon rules

Je - ho - vah rules the world in state, Je -

Je - ho - vah rules the world in state, Je -

MANOAH. HARAPHA. MANOAH.

Da - gon, Je - ho - vah rules the world in state, Great Da - gon rules, Je -

D *ff*

the world in state. His thunder roars,

ff

- ho - vah rules the world in state, His thunder roars,

ff

- ho - vah rules the world in state. His thunder roars,

CHORUS. *ff*

- ho - vah rules the world in state His thunder roars,

D

ff

heav'n shakes, His thun- der roars, . . .
heav'n shakes, His thun- der roars,
heav'n shakes, His thun- der roars, roars, . .
heav'n shakes, His thun- der roars, ...
roars, ... heav'n shakes, and
roars, ... heav'n shakes, and
. . roars, . - . . heav'n shakes, and
. . . . heav'n shakes, and
earth's a - ghast, His thun- der roars, heav'n shakes,
E
earth's a - ghast, His thun - der roars, heav'n shakes,
earth's a - ghast, His thun - der roars, heav'n shakes,
earth's a - ghast, His thun- der roars, heav'n shakes,
E

and earth is a - ghast, and earth is a - ghast.
and earth is a - ghast, and earth is a - ghast.
and earth is a - ghast, and earth is a - ghast.
and earth is a - ghast, and earth is a - ghast.
The stars, with deep a - - maze,
The stars, with deep a - - maze,
The stars, with deep a - - maze,
The stars, with deep a - - maze,
Re - - main in sted - - fast gaze, in sted - fast
Re - - main in sted - - fast gaze, in sted - fast
Re - - main in sted - - fast gaze, in sted - fast
Re - - main in sted - - fast gaze, in sted - fast

F
gaze; Great Da - gon is of Gods the
gaze; Je - ho - vah, Je - ho - vah is of Gods the
gaze; Je - ho - vah, Je - ho - vah is of Gods the
MANOAH. HARAPHA. MANOAH. CHORUS.
gaze; Je - ho - vah, Great Da - gon is, Je - ho - vah is of Gods the
F
G
first and last,
first and last, is of Gods . . . .
first and last, is of Gods . . .
first and last,
G
is of Gods . . .
the first and last, . . the first and last, is of Gods the first
. . . . the first and last, . . . the first
is of Gods . . . . the first

H
the first
and last, the first, the first
and last, the first the first
and last, the first, the first
H
and last, the first and last,
of Gods the first and last,
of Gods the first and last, Je-
of Gods the first and last, Je-
MANOAH.
of Gods the first and last, Je-
ff
f

Great Da - gon is
of
- ho - vah,
Je - ho - vah is
of
- ho - vah,
Je - ho - vah is
of
Harapha.
Manoah.
Chorus.
- ho - vah,
Great Da - gon is,
Je - ho - vah is
of
Gods . . .
the first
and last.
Gods . . .
the first
and last.
Gods . . .
the first
and last.
Gods . .
the first
and last.
Ped.

PART III.

No. 68. RECITATIVE.—"MORE TROUBLE IS BEHIND."

SAMSON.
show Some pub-lic proof, to grace this so-lemn feast." I am an He-brew, and our law for-
HARAPHA.
-bids My pre-sence at their vain re-li-gious rites. This an-swer will of-fend;
SAMSON.
re-gard thy-self. My-self! my conscience and in-ter-nal peace! Am I so broke with
ser-vi-tude, to yield To such ab-surd commands? to be their fool, And play be-fore their
HARAPHA.
god? I will not come. My message, given with speed, brooks no de-lay.

No. 69.
AIR.—"PRESUMING SLAVE."
HARAPHA.
Pomposo.
VOICE.
PIANO.
♪ = 112.
f
p
Pre - sum - ing slave, pre - sum - ing slave! . . to
move their wrath! For . . mer - cy sue, Or . . vengeance due Dooms in one
fa - - - tal word thy death. Pre - sum - ing slave!
A
For . . mer - cy sue, Or . . vengeance due Dooms in one fa - tal word thy death,
dooms in one fa - - - - - - - - - tal word thy death!
B

p
Pre - sum - ing slave, pre - sum - ing slave! Con -
- si - der, ere it be too late, To ward th'un - err - - ing shaft of
C
C
fate, to ward th'un - err - - ing shaft of fate, Con - si - der, ere it
be too late, To ward th'un - err - ing shaft of fate, to ward th'un -
- err - - - - - ing shaft . . . . of fate, Con

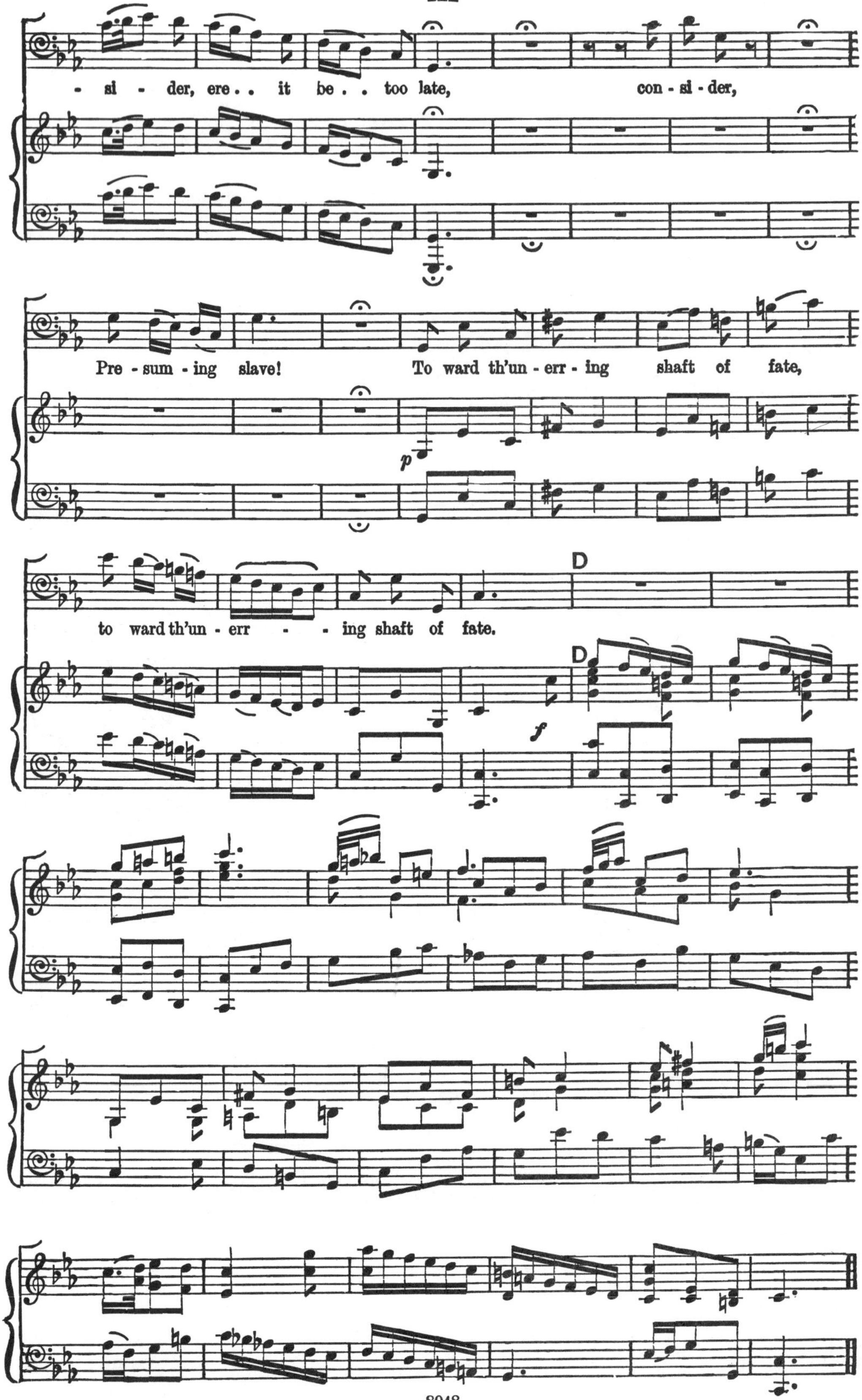
- si - der, ere . . it be . . too late, con - si - der,
Pre - sum - ing slave! To ward th'un - err - ing shaft of fate,
p
to ward th'un - err - - ing shaft of fate.
D
D
f

STAND

No. 70. RECITATIVE.—"CONSIDER, SAMSON."

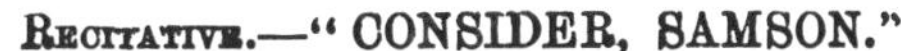

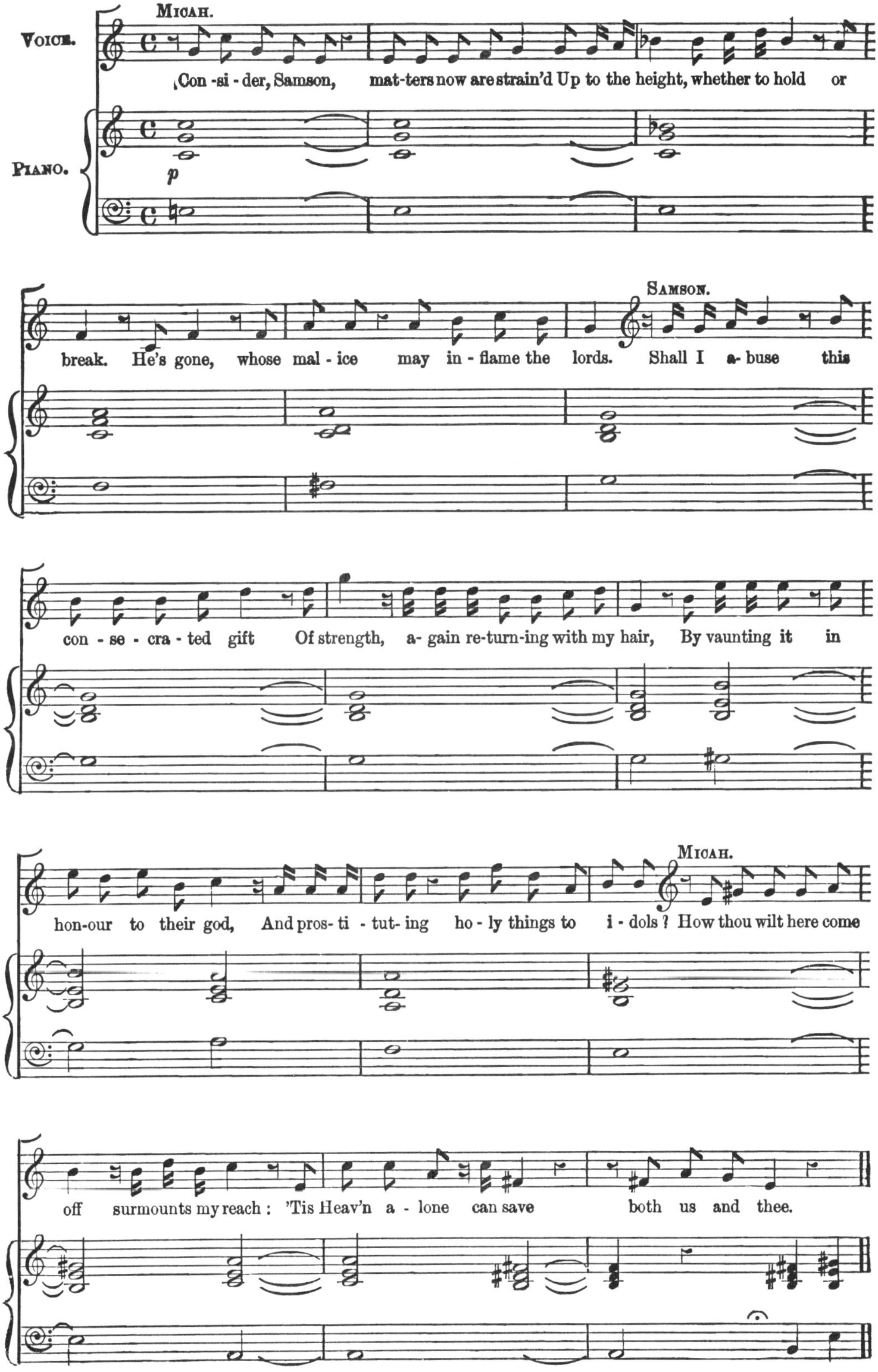
VOICE.
PIANO.
MICAH.
p
Con-si-der, Samson, mat-ters now are strain'd Up to the height, whether to hold or
break. He's gone, whose mal-ice may in-flame the lords.
SAMSON.
Shall I a-buse this
con-se-cra-ted gift Of strength, a-gain re-turn-ing with my hair, By vaunting it in
hon-our to their god, And pros-ti-tut-ing ho-ly things to i-dols?
MICAH.
How thou wilt here come
off surmounts my reach: 'Tis Heav'n a-lone can save both us and thee.

No. 71.
Chorus.—"WITH THUNDER ARMED."
Vivace.
Soprano.
Alto.
Tenor.
Bass.
With thun-der arm'd, with thun-der arm'd, great God, a - rise, a - rise, a - rise, great God, a - rise, with thun - der arm'd, with thun- der arm'd, great God. a -
With thun-der arm'd, with thun-der arm'd, great God, a - rise, a - rise, a - rise, great God, a - rise, with thun - der
With thun-der arm'd, with thun-der arm'd, great God, a - rise, a - rise, a - rise, great God, a - rise, with thun- der arm'd, with thun- der arm'd, great God, a -
With thun-der arm'd, with thun-der arm'd, great God, a - rise, a - rise, a - rise, great God, a - rise, with thun - der
Vivace.
Piano.
♩ = 76.
f
8048.

A
-rise, with thun - der arm'd, great God, a - rise, a - rise;
mf
arm'd, with thun - der arm'd, great God, a - rise, a - rise; Help,
-rise, with thun - der arm'd, great God, a - rise, a - rise;
arm'd, . . . great God, a - rise, a - rise;
A
p
p
Help, Lord,
cres.
Lord, or Is - rael's champion dies,
p
Help,
p
Help,
cres.
or Israel's champion dies!
B f
with thunder arm'd, with thunder
f
with thunder arm'd, with thunder
cres.
f
Lord, or Israel's champion dies! with thun-der
cres.
f
Lord, or Israel's champion dies! with thunder arm'd, with thunder
B
f

arm'd, great God, a - rise, with thun - der arm'd, with thun-der arm'd, great God, a -
arm'd, great God, a - rise, with thun - der arm'd, with thun-der arm'd, great God, a -
arm'd, great God, a - rise, with thun - der arm'd, with thun-der arm'd, great God, a -
arm'd, great God, a - rise, with thun - der arm'd, with thun-der arm'd, great God, a -
- rise; Help,
- rise; Help,
- rise; Help, Lord, or Is - rael's cham-pion
- rise; Help, Lord, or Is - rael's cham-pion
p
cres.
ritard.
dim.
Lord, or Is - - - - rael's cham - pion
Lord, or Is - rael's champion dies, or Is - rael's cham - pion
dies, or Is -rael's champion dies, or Is - rael's cham - pion
dies, or Is - rael's cham pion

tempo.
Fine.
D
dies; To Thy pro-tec-tion
dies; To Thy pro-tec-tion
dies; To Thy pro-tec-tion
dies; To Thy pro-tec - -
tempo.
Fine.
D
this Thy ser - vant take, And save, O save us,
this Thy ser - vant take, And save, O save us,
this Thy ser - vant take, And save, and save, O save us,
- - tion this Thy ser - vant take,
D.C.
and save, O save, O save us for Thy ser-vant's sake.
O save . . . us for Thy ser - vant's sake.
O . . . . save us for Thy ser-vant's sake.
And save, O save . . us for Thy ser - vant's sake.
D.C.

No. 72

RECITATIVE.—"BE OF GOOD COURAGE."

Samson.
Let but that Spi-rit (which first rush'd on me In the camp of Dan) inspire me at my need: Then shall I
make Je - ho-vah's glo - ry known: Their i - dol gods shall
from His presence fly, Scatter'd like
sheep be - fore the God of Hosts.
f
ff

No. 73.

Air.—"THUS WHEN THE SUN."

Andante.

Voice.

Andante.

Piano.

♪ = 116.

mf

cres.

f

p

tr

f

pp

A Samson.

Thus when the sun in's wa - t'ry bed, All cur- tain'd with a cloud - y red,

A

mp

p

Pil - lows his chin up - on an o- rient wave, ...

pil - lows his chin up-on an o - rient wave,
up - on an o - - rient wave;
B
cres.
f
The wan-d'ring sha - dows, ghast - ly pale, All troop to their in -
tr
p
fer - nal jail, Each fet - ter'd ghost slips to his sev' - ral grave,
slips to his sev' - ral grave,
C

each fet - ter'd ghost slips to his sev' - ral grave, The
wan - d'ring sha - dows, ghast - ly . . pale, All troop to their in - fer - nal jail, Each
fet - - - - - - - ter'd ghost slips to his sev' - ral grave, each
p
cres.
fet - ter'd ghost slips to his sev' - ral grave,
Adagio.
D Tempo 1mo.
pp
f
tr
p
f

No. 74. RECITATIVE.—"WITH MIGHT ENDUED."

No. 75. AIR.—"THE HOLY ONE OF ISRAEL."

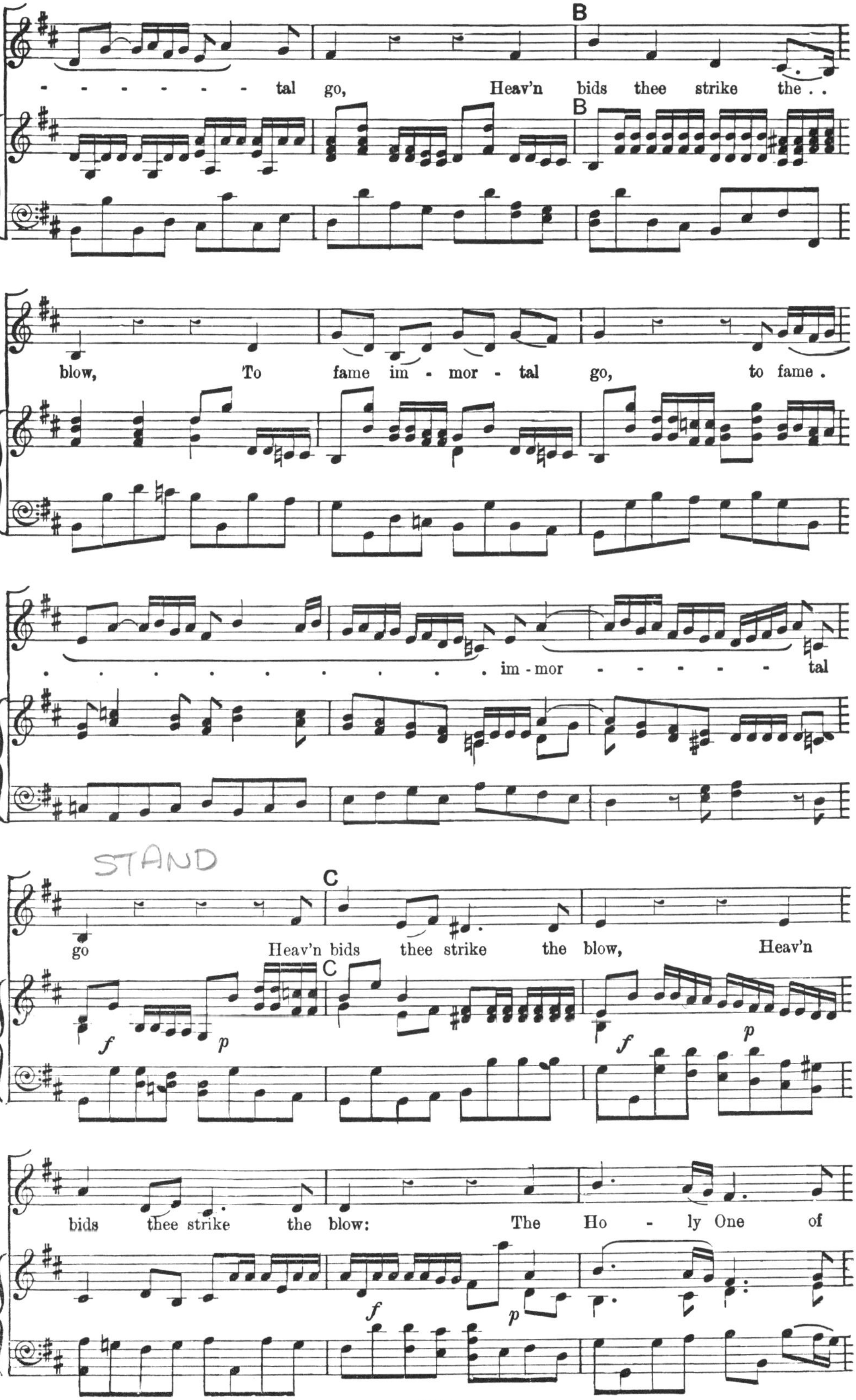
B
tal go, Heav'n bids thee strike the . .
B
blow, To fame im - mor - tal go, to fame .
. im - mor - - - - - - - tal
STAND
C
go Heav'n bids thee strike the blow, Heav'n
C
f p f p
bids thee strike the blow: The Ho - ly One of
f p

K

Is - - rael is thy guide, the Ho - - - - -
- - - - - - ly One of Is - ra - el is thy
No. 76. Chorus.—“TO FAME IMMORTAL GO.”
Allegro.
Soprano.
Alto.
Tenor.
Bass.
Piano.
= 168.
To fame, to
Chorus.
guide.
To fame, to
To fame, to
To fame, to
fame im - mor - tal go, to fame im - mor - tal go, Heav'n
fame im - mor - tal go, to fame im - mor - tal go, Heav'n
fame im - mor - tal go, to fame im - mor - tal go, Heav'n
fame im - mor - tal go, to fame im - mor - tal go, Heav'n

A
bids thee strike the blow, go, go,
bids thee strike the blow, go, go,
bids thee strike the blow, go, go, The
bids thee strike the blow, go, go, The
A
The Ho - ly One of . .
The Ho - ly One of . .
Ho - ly One of . . Is - rael is thy guide;
Ho - ly One of . . Is - rael is thy guide;
f
mf
B
Is - rael is thy . . guide: Heav'n bids thee strike the
Is - rael is thy . . guide: Heav'n bids thee strike the
Heav'n bids thee strike the
Heav'n bids thee strike the
B
f

blow: The Ho - ly One of Is - rael is thy
blow: The Ho - ly One of Is - rael is thy
blow: The Ho - ly One of Is - rael is thy
blow: The Ho - ly One of Is - rael is thy

guide, the Ho - ly One of Is - rael is thy
guide, the Ho - ly One of Is - rael is thy
guide, the Ho - ly One of Is - rael is thy
guide, the Ho - ly One of Is - rael is thy

guide.
guide.
guide.
guide.

mp

No. 77. Recitative.—"OLD MANOAH, WITH YOUTHFUL STEPS."

No. 78. Air—"GREAT DAGON HAS SUBDUED OUR FOE."

boast - ed he - ro low,
Great Da - gon
has . . sub- dued our foe, And brought their boast - ed he - ro low;
B
Sound out his power . . . . . . in notes di - vine, ...
. . Praise him with mirth, . . high cheer, and wine, praise him with mirth, . .
high cheer, and wine, praise him with mirth, high cheer and wine,
C
f
p

Sound out his
p
power in notes di - vine, praise him with mirth, . . high cheer, and wine. Great
Da - gon has . . sub - dued our foe, And brought their boast - ed he - ro
D
low.
D
f
Sound out his power
mf
in notes di - vine, sound out His power in notes di - vine, Praise him with
p

mirth, high cheer, and wine, ...
p
praise him with mirth, . . high cheer, and wine,
E
E
f
Sound out his power in notes di - vine, praise him with mirth, high
p
cheer, and wine, ...
praise him with mirth, high cheer, and wine!
f

No. 79 CHORUS.—"GREAT DAGON HAS SUBDUED OUR FOE."

power, ... sound out his power, ...

Sound out his power, sound out his power, . . .

Sound out his power, ... sound out his

Sound out his power, ...

. . . in notes di - vine, Praise him with mirth, high cheer, and

. . . in notes di - vine, Praise him with mirth, high cheer, and

power, . . . in notes di - vine, Praise him with mirth,

sound out his power in notes di - vine, Praise him with mirth,

wine, praise him with mirth, praise him with mirth, high cheer, and

wine, praise him with mirth, praise him with mirth, high cheer, and

high cheer, and wine, praise him, praise him with mirth, high cheer, and

high cheer, and wine, praise him, praise him with mirth, high cheer, and

B
wine.
wine.
wine.
wine.
B
f
Sound out his power in notes di - vine, Praise him with
Sound out his power in notes di - vine, Praise him with
Sound out his power in notes di - vine, Praise him with
Sound out his power in notes di - vine, Praise him with
cres.
ff

C
mirth, high cheer, and wine, Great Da - gon has sub - dued our
mirth, high cheer, and wine, Great Da - gon has sub - dued . . our
mirth, high cheer, and wine, Great Da - gon has sub - dued our
mirth, high cheer, and wine, Great Da - gon has sub - dued . . our
C
D
foe, And brought their boast - ed he - ro low,
foe, And brought their boast - ed he - ro low,
foe, And brought their boast - ed he - ro low,
foe, And brought their boast - ed he - ro low, Sound out his
D
f
Sound out his power, ...
Sound out his power, his power, . . . sound out his
Sound out his power, ... sound out his power,
power, ... sound out his power, sound out his

ff
sound out his power, sound, sound, sound, sound out his
power, sound, sound, sound, sound, sound out his
sound out his power, sound, sound, sound, sound out his
power, sound, sound, sound, sound, sound out his
power, in notes di - vine, Praise him with mirth, high cheer, and
power, in notes di - vine, Praise him with mirth, high cheer, and
power, in notes di - vine, Praise him with mirth, high cheer, and
power, in notes di - vine, Praise him with mirth high cheer, and
wine,
wine,
wine.
wine.

E
Sound out his power . . in notes di - vine, Praise him with
Sound out his power . . in notes di - vine, Praise him with
Sound out his power . . in notes di - vine, Praise him with
Sound out his power in notes di - vine, Praise him with
E
ff
mirth, . . high cheer, . . and wine, . . . praise him with mirth, . . high
mirth, . . high cheer, . . and wine, . . . praise him with mirth, . . high
mirth, . . high cheer, . . and wine, . . . praise him with mirth, . . high
mirth, . . high cheer, . . and wine, . . . praise him with mirth, . . high
cheer, and wine.
cheer, and wine.
cheer, and wine.
cheer, and wine.

No. 80.

RECITATIVE.—"WHAT NOISE OF JOY WAS THAT?"

No. 81. AIR.—"HOW WILLING MY PATERNAL LOVE."

B
Though wand'ring in the shades of night, Whilst I have eyes he
B
p
wants no light, Tho' wand'ring in the shades of night, . . Whilst I have eyes, . . he
C
wants no light, whilst I have eyes, . . he wants no light, whilst
C
pp
I have eyes, he wants no light.
tr
tr
f
p

No. 82. Recitative.—"YOUR HOPES OF HIS DELIVERY."
Micah.
Voice.
Your hopes of his de - liv' - ry seem not vain, In which all Israel's friends par - ti - ci - pate.
Piano.
p
Manoah.
I know your friend - ly minds, and—
No. 83. SINFONIA.
Presto.
Piano.
♩ = 120.
ff
ff sempre.
No. 84. Recitative.—"HEAVEN! WHAT NOISE?"
Manoah.
Voice.
Heav'n! what noise? Hor - ri - bly loud, un - like the for - mer shout.
Piano.
p

No. 85.
Chorus.—"HEAR US, OUR GOD."
Presto.
Soprano.
Alto.
Tenor.
Bass.
Hear us, our
Presto.
Piano.
♩ = 120.
O hear us, our God!
O hear us, our God!
Hear us, our God! hear us.
God! hear us, O hear our cry, . .
O hear our cry! death! ru - in! fall'n!
O hear our cry! death! ru - in! fall'n!
O hear our cry! death! ru - in!
. . . hear our cry! death! ru - in!
A

no help is nigh:
O mer - cy, heav'n,
fall'n,
no help is nigh, no help, O . . mer - cy,
fall'n, no help is nigh,
O mer - cy, heav'n,
fall'n, no help is nigh,
O mer - cy, heav'n,
we sink, we
dim.
heav'n, we sink, we die,
we sink, we die,
O mer - cy, we sink, we die,
dim.
con 8ve.
B
cres.
die, O, O mer - cy, heav'n, O . . .
O mer - cy, heav'n, O . . .
O mer - cy, O mer - cy,
f
cres.
f
con 8ve.

mer-cy, heav'n, no help is nigh, we
mer-cy, heav'n, no help is nigh,
O mer-cy, heav'n, no help is nigh,
O mer-cy, heav'n, no help is nigh,
C
dim.
sink, O mer-cy, heav'n, we sink, we die,
O mer-cy, heav'n, we die, we sink, we die,
we sink, we die, we sink, we die,
we sink, we die, we sink, we die,
p
pp
O, we die!
O, we die!
O, we die!
O, we die!

No. 86. RECITATIVE.—"WHERE SHALL I RUN."

once he did de-stroy, and was de-stroy'd. The e-di-fice (where all were met to see) Up-on their
heads and on his own he pull'd.
MANOAH.
O last-ly o-ver-strong a-gainst thy-self! A
dread-ful way thou took'st to thy re-venge, Glo-rious, yet dear-ly bought.
p
No. 87.
AIR.—"YE SONS OF ISRAEL."
VOICE.
Largo assai.
MICAH.
Ye sons of Is-rael, now la-
Largo assai.
p
pp
PIANO.
♪ = 72.
-ment; Your spear is . . broke, your bow un-bent: Your glo-ry's fled;
p

Amongst the dead Great Samson lies: For ev-er, for ev-er, for
pp
ev - er, ev - er clos'd his eyes!
A
Your glo-ry's.. fled;
A
p
Amongst the dead Great Samson lies: For ev-er, for ev-er, ev - er clos'd.. his
eyes, for ev-er, for ev-er clos'd . . . . his eyes,
for ev-er, for ev - - - - - er clos'd.. his eyes.

No. 89 omitted.

DEAD MARCH. (No. 1.)

No. 91. DEAD MARCH.* (No. 2.)

* Dead March from "Saul."

No. 92 OMITTED.

No. 93.
Chorus and Soli.—"GLORIOUS HERO."
Largo.
Soprano.
Alto.
Tenor.
Bass.
Manoah.
Glorious he - ro, may thy grave Peace and hon - our ev - er
Largo.
mf
p
Piano.
♪ = 76.
have; Af - ter all thy pains and woes, Rest e - ter - nal, rest e - ter - nal, sweet re - pose! . . .
mp
Glo-rious
mp
Glo-rious
mp
A
An Israelitish Woman.
The vir-gins, too, shall on their feast-ful
he - ro, may thy grave Peace and hon - our ev - er have.
he - ro, may thy grave Peace and hon - our ev - er have.
A
pp

days Vis - it his tomb with flow'rs, and there bewail His lot, un-for - tunate in nuptial choice.

B CHORUS OF VIRGINS.

mf

Bring the lau - rels, bring the bays, Strew his hearse, and strew the ways, Bring the lau -rels, bring the

mf

Bring the lau-rels, bring the bays, Strew his hearse, and strew the ways, Bring the lau -rels, bring the

B

mf

bays, Strew his hearse, strew his hearse, and strew the ways.

bays, Strew his hearse, strew his hearse, and strew the ways.

C AN ISRAELITISH WOMAN.

Adagio.

May ev' - ry he - ro fall like

C *Adagio.*

thee, Through sor - row to fe - li - ci-ty, through sor - row to fe - li - ci-ty,

May ev'-ry he-ro fall like thee, Through sor-row to fe-li-ci-ty!
Tempo 1mo.
D
Chorus of Virgins.
mf
Bring the lau-rels, bring the bays, Strew his hearse, and strew the ways, Bring the lau-rels, bring the bays, Strew his hearse, strew his hearse, and strew the ways!
Bring the lau-rels, bring the bays, Strew his hearse, and strew the ways, Bring the lau-rels, bring the bays, Strew his hearse, strew his hearse, and strew the ways!
D Tempo 1mo.
cres.
E Chorus.
f
Glo-rious he-ro, may thy grave Peace and hon-our ev-er have; Af-ter all thy pains and
E

mp
woes, Rest e-ter-nal, sweet re-pose, . . rest e-ter-nal, sweet re-pose, rest e-
woes, Rest e-ter-nal, sweet re-pose, . . rest e-ter-nal, sweet re-pose, rest e-
woes, Rest e-ter-nal, sweet re-pose, rest e-ter-nal, sweet re-pose, rest e-
woes, Rest e-ter-nal, sweet re-pose, ... rest e-
-ter-nal, sweet re-pose, rest e-ter-nal, After all thy pains and
-ter-nal, sweet re-pose, sweet re-pose, rest e-ter-nal, Af-ter all thy
-ter-nal, sweet re-pose, rest e-ter-nal, rest e-ter-nal, Af-ter
-ter-nal, sweet re-pose, . . sweet re-pose, rest e-ter
F
mf
woes, . . . af-ter all thy pains and woes, Rest e-ter-nal, rest e-
pains . . . . . . and woes, Rest e-ter-nal, rest e-
all . . . thy pains and woes, Rest e-ter-nal, rest e-
-nal, Af-ter all thy pains and woes, Rest e-ter-nal, rest e-
p

- ter - nal, sweet re - pose!

- ter - nal, sweet re - pose!

- ter - nal, . sweet re - pose!

- ter - nal, sweet re - pose!

pp

No. 94. Recitative.—"COME COME: NO TIME FOR LAMENTATION NOW."

No. 95.

AIR.—"LET THE BRIGHT SERAPHIM."

Andante.

HANDEL.

VOICE.

Andante.

PIANO.
♩ = 76.

f

A

Let the bright Se - ra - phim in

A

p

burn - ing row,

f

Their loud up - lift - ed

An-gel-trumpets blow,
f
B
Let the bright Se-ra-phim in burn - ing row, in
B
f
p
burn - ing, burn - - - - - ing row, Their loud up - lift-ed An-gel -
p
tr
- trum - pets blow, ... their loud up - lift-ed An-gel -
- trum - pets blow, ...

C
their
loud, ... their loud up - lift - ed An - gel -
- trump - ets blow,
D
Let the bright Se - ra-phim in burn - ing row, in
burn - ing, burn - - - ing row, Their loud up - lift - ed
E
mf
p
f

Angel-trumpets blow, their loud . . up-lift - - ed Angel-trumpets blow, . . .
. . . . their loud . . up-lift-ed Angel-
mf
p
F
. trum-pets blow:
F
f
STAND
G
Let the Che-ru-bic host, in tune - - ful choirs, Touch
G
p

their im-mor-tal harps . . with gold - en wires, Let the Che-ru-bic host, in

tune - ful choirs, Touch their im-mor-tal harps, touch their im-mor-tal harps . . .

. . . . with gold - en wires, ...

. . . . touch their im-mor-tal harps . . with gold - en

wires.

cres. *f*

No. 96. Chorus.—LET THEIR CELESTIAL CONCERTS ALL UNITE

A
To sound His praise, ... Let their ce - les-tial con-certs
Let their ce - les-tial con-certs
. . . . in end-less morn of light, Let their ce - les-tial con-certs
Let their ce - les-tial con-certs
A
all u - nite, let their ce - les- tial con - certs all u - nite,
all u - nite, let their ce - les- tial con - certs all u - nite,
all u - nite, let their ce - les- tial con - certs all u - nite,
all u - nite, let their ce - les- tial con - certs all u - nite, To sound His
Ev - er, . . ev - er, . . ev - er to sound His praise in end - less
Ev - er, ev - er, ev - er to sound His praise in end - less
Ev - er, ev - er, ev - er to sound His praise in end - less
praise . . . . in end - less

B
morn of light, to sound His praise, ... to
morn of light, ev - er, ev - er ev - er to sound, to
morn of light, ev - er, ev - er, ev - er to sound. to
morn of light, ev - er, ev - er, ev - er to sound, to
B
sound His praise in end-less morn, . . . in end - less, end - less morn of light,
sound His praise in end-less morn, . . . in end-less, end - less morn of light,
sound His praise in end-less morn of light, in end-less, end - less morn of light,
sound His praise in end-less morn, in end - less, end - less morn of light,
C
Let their ce - les- tial con-certs all u - nite, let their ce - les- tial con-certs
Let their ce - les- tial con-certs all u - nite,
Let their ce - les- tial con-certs all u - nite, To sound His praise, ...
Let their ce - les- tial con-certs all u - nite,
C

all u-nite, Ev - er to sound, to sound His praise, ... to
let their ce-lestial concerts all u-nite, To sound His praise,
in end - less
let their celestial concert
sound His praise, ev - er, ev - er to sound His praise in
to sound His praise . . . . . . in end - -
morn of light, to sound His praise . . . . . .
all u - nite, ev - er to sound His
end - - - - less morn of light, Let their ce - les-tial con-certs all u - nite,
- - - - - - less morn of light, Let their ce - les- tial con-certs all u - nite,
. . . . . in end-less morn of light, Let their ce - les-tial con-certs all u - nite,
praise . . . in end-less morn of light, Let their ce - les- tial con-certs all u - nite,
ff

D
let their ce-les-tial concerts all u-nite,
let their ce-les-tial concerts all u-nite,
let their ce-les-tial concerts all u-nite, Ev - - - - - - - - - er to
let their ce-les-tial concerts all u-nite, Ev - er, ev - er, ev - er, ev - er to
D
ff
Ev - er, .. ev - er to sound . . . .
Ev - er to sound . . . . . . His praise in end - less
sound, to sound His praise in end - - - - less
sound His praise . . . . . . in end - less
. . His praise, ev - er to sound, to sound His praise in
morn of light, ev - er to sound, to sound His praise in
morn of light, ev - er to sound, to sound His praise in
morn of light, in end-less morn, ... in
E

end - less morn . . . . of light, ... in end - less morn of light,
end - less morn . . . . of light, ... in end - less morn of light,
end - less morn . . . . of light, ... in end - less morn of light,
end - less morn . . . . of light, ... in end - less morn of light,
Let their ce - les - tial con - certs all u - nite,
Let their ce - les - tial con - certs all u - nite,
ff
ff
Ev - er to sound, to sound His praise in end - less morn . . . .
Ev - er to sound, to sound His praise in end - less morn . . . .
Ev - er to sound, to sound His praise in end - less morn . . .
Ev - er to sound . . His praise . . . . in end - less morn . . . .
ff

Printed and bound in Great Britain by
Caligraving Limited Thetford Norfolk

5/99 (34125)

INDEX.

PART THE FIRST.

PART THE SECOND.

PART THE THIRD.

CHORAL WORKS FOR MIXED VOICES

BACH
CHRISTMAS ORATORIO
For soprano, alto, tenor & bass soli, SATB & orchestra
MASS IN B MINOR
For two sopranos, alto, tenor & bass soli, SSATB & orchestra
ST MATTHEW PASSION
For soprano, alto, tenor & bass soli, SATB & orchestra

BRAHMS
REQUIEM
For soprano & baritone soli, SATB & orchestra

ELGAR
GIVE UNTO THE LORD PSALM 29
For SATB & organ or orchestra

FAURE
ed Desmond Ratcliffe
REQUIEM
For soprano & baritone soli, SATB & orchestra

HANDEL
ed Watkins Shaw
MESSIAH
For soprano, alto, tenor & bass soli, SATB & orchestra

HAYDN
CREATION
For soprano, tenor & bass soli, SATB & orchestra
IMPERIAL 'NELSON' MASS
For soprano, alto, tenor & bass soli, SATB & orchestra
MARIA THERESA MASS
For soprano, alto, tenor & bass soli, SATB & orchestra
MASS IN TIME OF WAR 'PAUKENMESSE'
For soprano, alto, tenor & bass soli,i SATB & orchestra

MONTEVERDI
ed Denis Stevens & John Steele
BEATUS VIR
For soloists, double choir, organ & orchestra
ed John Steele
MAGNIFICAT
For SSATB chorus, instruments & organ
ed Denis Stevens
VESPERS
For soloists, double choir, organ & orchestra

MOZART
REQUIEM MASS
For soprano, alto, tenor & bass soli, SATB & orchestra

SCARLATTI
ed John Steele
DIXIT DOMINUS
For SATB, soli & chorus, string orchestra & organ continuo

901 (90)